POSITIVE **BUSINESS**

Master Change,
Maximize **Success**

POSITIVE **BUSINESS**

Master Change,
Maximize **Success**

Effective Strategies for Realizing Your Goals

By Rebecca Potts and
Jeanenne LaMarsh

CHRONICLE BOOKS
SAN FRANCISCO

First published in the United States in 2004 by Chronicle Books LLC.

Copyright © 2004 by Duncan Baird Publishers
Text copyright © 2004 by Rebecca Potts and Jeanenne LaMarsh
Commissioned artwork copyright © 2004 by Duncan Baird Publishers

Conceived, created, and designed by Duncan Baird Publishers Ltd.

Library of Congress Cataloging-in-Publication Data available.

ISBN 0-8118-4170-7

Manufactured in Singapore

Managing Editors: Judy Barratt with Julia Charles
Editors: Ingrid Court-Jones with Joanne Clay
Managing Designer: Manisha Patel
Designer: Suzanne Tuhrim
Commissioned artwork: Melvyn Evans and Jud Guitteau

Typeset in Bembo

Distributed in Canada by
Raincoast Books
9050 Shaughnessy Street
Vancouver, British Columbia V6P 6E5

10 9 8 7 6 5 4 3 2 1

Chronicle Books LLC
85 Second Street
San Francisco, California 94105

www.chroniclebooks.com

PUBLISHER'S NOTE
To avoid the cumbersome repetition of "he or she" and "his or her,"
this book breaks from traditional grammatical convention in using
"they" or "their" when referring to, for example, "a sponsor,"
"a change agent" or "a target."

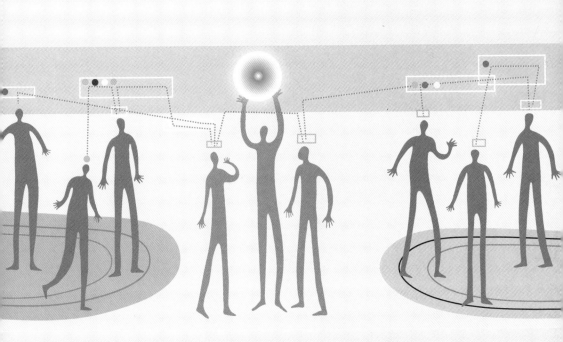

To our colleagues at LaMarsh and Associates
for all the support they gave and the patience
they showed while we were writing this book,
and for the knowledge they contribute daily
to our understanding of the change process.

CONTENTS

There is a running joke among colleagues at LaMarsh and Associates that our brains are not made up of brain cells, but of filters. This is because we filter every situation that faces us or our clients, by applying the change process to see whether the situation has change implications. The objectivity we gain from the change process gives us a simple yet powerful tool to help us understand and analyze any change situation.

We wrote this book to help you deal successfully with change in a business environment, whether you wish to implement a large-scale change that will affect a huge corporation or reorganize three people in a corner of your department. In the following pages we show how adaptable and practical change management can be and tell you about some of our experiences with changes both large and small. Once you have mastered the lessons of this book, you will be able to plan and tailor your own changes, whatever their size.

The change process was pioneered in the early 1980s when leadership was a big buzzword in the business community. At that time leadership seminars were held everywhere, countless books were written on the subject, and every business consultant advocated leadership skills as the key to success. In retrospect, we see that all the fuss about leadership was really about change. When sexual harassment emerged as a leadership issue in the United States, Jeanenne LaMarsh worked relentlessly to address this problem. She helped to bring about a fundamental change in workplace behavior and attitudes to sexual harassment. Her work on this issue and the changes she helped to bring about were the

genesis for many of the thoughts and experiences about change described in this book.

Over the last 25 years, we have had the opportunity to teach colleagues and clients a great deal about change management. We have helped to implement change successfully in the healthcare, manufacturing, technology and financial industries, to name but a few. Using this book, we hope that you, too, will learn the techniques of successful change management. And after you turn the last page, we challenge you to bring this topic full circle by sharing your experiences with us. Now let *us* learn from *you* – and change!

Rebecca Potts and Jeanenne LaMarsh

HOW TO USE THIS BOOK

No organization in the world can survive if it is the same today as it was yesterday. Your competitors are changing. Your customer is too. So is the world around you.

Every day your competitors make decisions about what to change and how to do it. Like you, they are trying to maintain a competitive edge. They are making many of the same changes that you are. So if everyone is making the same changes, what determines the winner, the organization that gets the orders, the customers and the opportunity to flourish? The answer is the organization that can make the change happen faster, easier, cheaper and better.

Once an organization makes a decision about what to change, it needs to educate and inspire the workforce to support the change. This can be difficult because often people's first reaction to the prospect of, say, using new technology or reporting to a different manager is to resist and fight the change. Anticipating that potential resistance, determining how serious a threat to your change that resistance could be, and figuring out how to reduce the potential and/or actual resistance to your change is what this book is all about. By working systematically through the action steps we describe, within the Work Solutions, you will learn everything you need to do to make your change successful.

Chapters 1 to 4 tackle the core issue of resistance: how to assess the potential for resistance to your change by gathering and analyzing the relevant information; how to discover where resistance might come from, how strong it might be and what to do about it. Chapter 5 shows you how to

develop the action plan to reduce or eliminate resistance. Chapter 6 discusses how best to implement that action plan during the change process. And Chapter 7 shows you how to sustain the change once it has happened.

The most effective way to use this book is to apply it to a real-life change situation – whether it's a change that you are facing now, or a change that you have experienced already. That way, the book becomes far more than a theoretical discussion about change – it becomes a change-management handbook. By learning how to deal with resistance, by going through each Work Solution and applying what you learn from it to your own change, you will acquire a fine grasp of change issues and how to handle them. You will also gain a greater understanding of the potential risks to your own change, and find yourself ideally placed to reduce those risks by taking the appropriate action. Start now – the journey toward managing change for success begins here!

chapter 1

CHANGE – THE BASICS

In the twenty-first century, the pace of life is relentlessly fast. An event, a decision or even a rumor started in one part of the world can have an almost instant impact across the globe, thanks to the speed of email and satellite communication. This is particularly true in business, where markets are volatile and millions of dollars can be gained or lost in minutes. In the commercial world, keeping pace means having to deal constantly with changing situations.

Change, then, is a fact of corporate life. And it is our attitude to change that can make the difference between business success or failure. Should we react to change when it happens or should we be more pro-active? The answer is that if we wish to maintain a competitive edge today we need actively to embrace change and even pre-empt it.

But how do we go about this? Before we can control change, we need to understand it. In this chapter we examine the basics, such as how change comes about and why change fails; we consider who directs change and whom it affects; and we learn how to take our first steps in managing change.

CHANGE IS DRIVEN

Change does not just happen: it is driven by a reason, a thought, an idea. The cause of change comes from one of two sources: either from *outside* or from *inside* the organization.

On a global scale, your organization might by affected from *outside* by external forces such as natural disasters, political events or new government regulations that force you to change your business methods. Closer to home, competition might become more intense (making your current costs unviable or your product suddenly out of date), or keeping up with new technology might fundamentally change the way you do business.

Other changes come from *within* your organization. Internal factors that drive change may stem from a problem that needs solving or a desire for continuous improvement. For example, budget cuts, interdepartmental conflict and the introduction of new computer systems can all bring

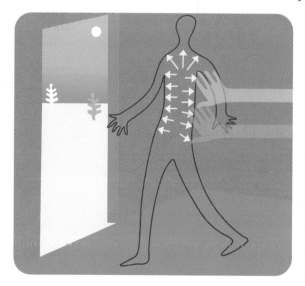

about changes that require employees to be more flexible about the type and amount of work they do.

Although you might not have noticed previously, change is already an integral part of your organization. The Work Solution opposite will help you to analyze how change impacts upon your present situation.

WORK SOLUTION 1

Analyzing the Current State of Change

Change is a constant – and it is happening now in your own organization. This exercise will help you to analyze its pace and character. (You will need a pen and some paper.)

1. Select a recent, typical change in your organization. Start by deciding whether the change was a major transformation or a minor adjustment. Now consider what drove that change. Were the drivers internal or external? Was there more than one driver? Follow the driver(s) back to their beginnings (you may find that there was an external change driver that gave rise to one or more internal change drivers). Jot down the chain of events that led up to this change.

2. Next, widen the scope of your thinking. Ask yourself whether there are many changes like this one going on now. Is the number of changes increasing? Are they also becoming more complex? Would you say that the changes are pre-emptive (one step ahead of the way things are now) or reactive (they only happen when forced)? How effective are the changes? How do you think the process of change could be better managed? Write down your answers.

3. Now consider your own role in these changes. What role do you currently have? How could you extend your role? How would you manage change within the organization? Again, write down your answers.

4. You now have a snapshot of change in your organization and your role in that change. Keep your answers somewhere handy so that you can refer back to them as you work through the rest of this book.

WHAT IS CHANGE MANAGEMENT?

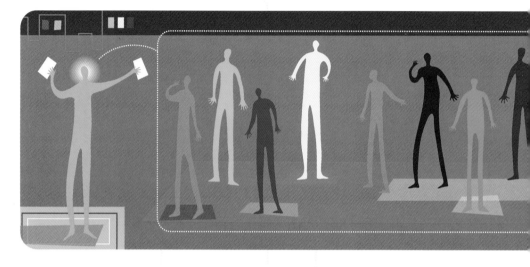

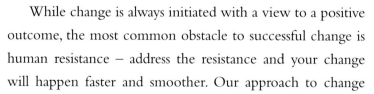

More and more organizations today choose to make frequent changes in order to survive in an increasingly competitive marketplace. Change management has evolved accordingly to offer tried-and-tested processes to help businesses carry out those changes successfully. However, there are many different approaches to change management.

We define change management as the systematic process of applying the knowledge, tools and resources needed to effect change to the people who will be impacted by it. The objective is to deliver the required business solution successfully in an organized, methodical way through managing the impact of change on the people involved.

While change is always initiated with a view to a positive outcome, the most common obstacle to successful change is human resistance – address the resistance and your change will happen faster and smoother. Our approach to change management has three primary functions. First, to identify who, among those who will be impacted by it, are likely to resist the change. Second, to assess the sources, types and degrees of resistance the change may encounter. And third, to design effective strategies to reduce that resistance.

By applying a change-management program you can predict the amount of resistance that may occur and the time and money required to deal with that resistance. This allows the people who have to implement the change to assess vital factors, such as whether the change is worth making and how successful it is likely to be.

Understanding why people resist change and how to overcome this resistance are at the core of our approach to change management. We will be examining these topics in depth and from many perspectives throughout the book.

THE KEY TO WELL-MANAGED CHANGE

Step 1: Identify resistance to the change
Address the five reasons why people resist change (see pp.20–22; see also pp.100–103)
Answer the eight essential questions to find out how much your change is likely to be resisted (see pp.24–5)

Step 2: Design ways to reduce that resistance
Draw up and implement:
• a communication plan (see pp.25, 114–19)
• a learning plan (see pp.26, 120–23)
• a reward plan (see pp.26, 124–9)

Step 3: Devise a master action plan
Control the implementation of the communication, learning and reward plans to ease the path of the change and to sustain the change once it has been completed (see pp.26–7)

THE CHANGE-MANAGEMENT MYTHS

As we have established, there are usually people within an organization who will resist change, and we know that this can undermine the overall success of change implementation. There are often also people who don't believe that managing change in a considered way is necessary. Usually, these are people in senior management who have the power and authority to decide how the change is managed, and their philosophy is: "Let's make it up as we go along." These managers tend to believe three myths about change and change management. Let's look at each in turn.

1. "People will always adapt to change."

We already know that this is not true. For all the reasons we give on pp.20–22, people will often resist change, even if it means the organization may suffer. Although we are a naturally adaptive species (being so has ensured our survival on this planet for thousands of years), we are also cautious.

2. "Our managers know how to manage change – it's what we pay them to do."

It's a commonly held belief among senior executives that managing change just happens automatically because there is management in place to oversee it. Many managers lack the necessary skills and training to manage change, and even if they have done the training and do have the skills, the chances are that they are so caught up in carrying out tasks on a day-to-day basis that structuring a change implementation program is the furthest thing from their minds.

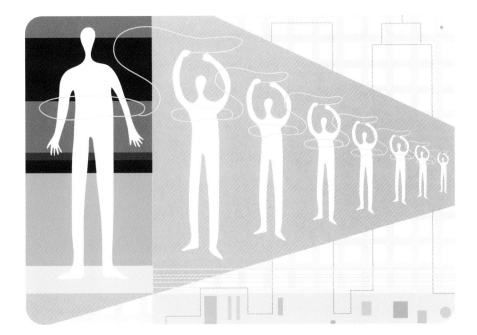

3. "Change happens: you don't have to manage it."

No! Too many factors can converge and sabotage the change. Studies show that, without change management, between 50 and 75 per cent of all manufacturing and technology change projects fail; and up to 75 per cent of all business re-structuring efforts do not produce the expected results. Experts are unanimous that it is crucial to manage people throughout change. Left to chance, change can be as detrimental to the organization as no change at all.

Because change does *not* just happen, it requires a solid framework that includes a plan and a process, as well as skilled people to design, implement and anticipate the implications of that plan and process.

LEARNING FROM PAST CHANGES

Have you ever worked on a change project that has not been successful? Have you ever been asked to implement a change and find yourself still working on it long after it should have been completed? If you can answer "yes" to either of these questions, read on. If you answered "no," skip to p.24.

Still with us? That's what we thought. As we have already established, internal and external change drivers give us the reasons for change (see pp.14–15). But making the change actually happen is another matter. If you want your change to be successful this time, it is useful to know where you went wrong before and what pitfalls you should avoid.

What are the most common reasons why change fails? The change might take too long to implement, cost too much, cause too much discomfort, and so on. Or, perhaps the organization makes the wrong decision in the first place. The decision regarding what change to make is critical – knowing which direction to take, which technology to buy, which market to enter, which organizational structure to choose requires skill, experience and knowledge of the business and its market trends. Most often, managers making the decisions about what change to make are smart people and the changes they propose are the right ones. But smart changes still fail. Why? Because, when faced with change, the people impacted by the change have a choice: they can either embrace the change willingly or choose to resist it. And too often, people take the latter option.

Now, let's look at the five basic reasons *why* people might choose to resist change. Maybe they don't want to leave the

current state – for example, they don't want to give up the way they have always worked, sitting with the same team they have always worked with, reporting to their current boss. Or, perhaps they don't want to go where the organization is going – literally, they don't wish to relocate; or they don't want to use the new technology or accept the new organizational culture. Then again, maybe they don't want to go through the process of changing, of learning how to do things the new way, of spending time juggling the new work with the old. Perhaps they don't see that there is a plan for the change, drawn up by people who know what they are doing, and who also know how to make the change happen. Or, maybe the people impacted by the change have been let down in the past, having committed to a previous change only to see it fail or be abandoned, or to find that the pain of the effort was greater than the positive result of the change.

These are some of the reasons why people resist change. Let's now explore how they show that resistance. A common way is through decreased productivity, while they spend time seeking information about the change or just complaining. Some people resist change by dragging their feet generally and trying to slow down the change as much as they possibly can. Others display no enthusiasm for learning or training in the new procedures. Some people even resist through increased absenteeism in an attempt to avoid the change process altogether; others are forced to take time off because they actually become ill from the stress of the change.

It is important never to underestimate the significance of resistance. First of all, resistance is contagious. It only takes one person to be frightened of the change and to express their fears to colleagues, and before you know it the misgivings have spread like wildfire. People talk to others they meet in the elevator, in the hallway, in the smoking area or in the cafeteria. Such conversations take their toll on productivity as more and more staff spend more and more time discussing their fears and less and less time working.

Second, resistance is paralyzing. If a worker is convinced that there is no good reason to make a certain change, that

things are just fine the way they are, they will not get much benefit from, say, the three-day training course scheduled for this week. While the trainer goes through the new procedure in minute detail, the worker will be thinking what a waste of time the whole exercise is and will not give the training their proper attention. The result will be that the training doesn't "take," so the time and money spent on it will have been completely wasted.

Third and lastly, resistance is obstructive. For example, say that in order to make the change happen your staff need new equipment. And for them to be able to use the new equipment, it must first be ordered and delivered. But the procurement people, who are frightened that the change will mean the elimination of their jobs, never quite get around to ordering the equipment, so, of course, it never arrives. The thinking behind this type of resistance is simple: without the new equipment there can be no change.

Resistance, whatever the cause and however it manifests itself, can have far-reaching consequences. Some employees might decide that they no longer wish to work for an organization that is going through frequent or difficult changes and they might opt to leave. (They might not admit that opposition to the change is their reason for leaving – they may say that they'd like to take early retirement or that they have found a better job.) But the bottom line is that staff who feel resistant often also feel alienated from the organization and if they leave, taking valuable knowledge and skills with them, the organization loses out.

ASSESSING AND REDUCING RESISTANCE

On page 17 we set out our Key to Well-Managed Change, which comprises three action steps that you need to follow in order to overcome resistance and implement the change successfully. Let's consider each in turn.

Step 1: Identify resistance to the change

We've already learned the five basic reasons *why* people might resist the change (see pp.20–22). Now let's list the eight key questions that you need to ask yourself to find out *how* your change will be resisted. By gathering information in this way, you will be able to identify who might resist this change, what form that resistance may take and what to do about it. (Each question is examined in detail later in the book on the pages cited below.)

• Question 1: *Why change?* Who might resist the change because they can't see why they have to change? (See pp.40–41.)

• Question 2: *Change to what?* Who might resist because of the nature of the change they are being asked to make? (See pp.40–45.)

• Question 3: *How will we change?* Who might resist because of the way the change is being handled? (See pp.48–51.)

• Question 4: *Who ordered this change?* The answer to this question could raise another: is the attitude of management toward this change causing resistance? (See pp.68–75.)

• Question 5: *Who is going to deliver this change?* Could a lack of skills or ability on the part of the people managing the change provide a source of resistance? (See pp.76–81.)

• Question 6: *Who is going to change?* And will the targets of all this change have the capability to change easily? (See pp.82–91.)

• Question 7: *Will this change be handled in the same way as the last one (and the one before that)?* This question prompts the examination of people's previous experiences of change, which might make them reluctant to support this change. (See pp.96–9.)

• Question 8: *How serious is the potential problem of resistance?* Putting all the information that you have gathered together, you now need to analyze whether your change is at risk and, if so, assess how seriously. (See pp.110–11.)

Step 2: Design ways to reduce that resistance

In our experience, resistance to change has been shown to decrease when you devise and implement the following three plans: a communication plan; a learning plan; and a reward plan. Let's look at the three plans in more detail.

Starting with the communication plan, it is vital to make sure that each person in the organization is provided with all the information that they need in order to make an informed choice about whether to support the change or to resist it. After all, let's not forget that people *do* have a choice. By providing true and accurate information in a straightforward, accessible way, you not only stop the spread of potentially damaging rumors but you also limit the amount of working time that people waste speculating about what is likely to happen. (See pp.114–19 for how to devise such a plan.)

Next, we have the learning plan. This ensures that everyone gets the opportunity to develop the skills and to acquire the knowledge they will need in order to survive the transition from the old order to the new order, and learn the new ways of doing business in the post-change state. Giving people the chance to gain new skills will also decrease the number of missed business opportunities that could occur because the organization's workforce lacks the right expertise. (For information on how to draw up a learning plan, see pp.120–23.)

Lastly, providing encouragement and support for employees' efforts to achieve the desired state through a reward plan will boost staff morale, which is important because change can cause upheaval. The current workers are more likely to embrace the change if you reward and support them through the change process. The plan will also ensure that fewer workers will want to leave and thus save the organization the costs of recruiting and training new employees. (To learn more about devising a reward plan, see pp.124–9.)

Step 3: Devise a master action plan

The data you collect to help you identify resistance to the change and the communication, learning and reward plans that you draw up are useful tools, but they are of no value whatsoever unless they deliver results. The best way to ensure this is to devise another plan – a master action plan – to give yourself an overview of when to do what. Timing is of the essence here. For example, before you implement the change, you need to give the workforce information about your proposals for the change; then you need to arrange any new training sessions so that your staff are equipped and ready to work the new way as soon as the change is made; meanwhile you must also ensure that you reward and reinforce the efforts employees make to support the change, both in the time while the change is happening, and also after it has been implemented.

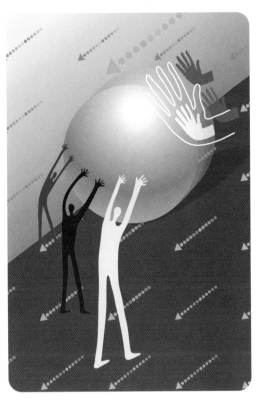

Putting into practice the Key to Well-Managed Change could be an expensive and time-consuming process because you will need extra resources in order to implement the change. As a result you will need a firm commitment from those who give the go-ahead (probably senior management) before you can start making the change happen. You need to convince them with solid data, such as an assessment of how the costs of making the change will be more than offset by the projected increases the change will produce. Then you, as the agent of this change, and your managers will be in a position to decide exactly what resources you need to allocate to ensure that the change not only happens, but happens smoothly.

CONTROLLING THE CHANGE PROCESS

The steps we have outlined for assessing and reducing resistance call for what is perhaps a more disciplined approach to managing change than your organization may have used previously. It might be apparent from our discussion so far that change management has a lot in common with project management – the science of setting up, testing and implementing the ideas and strategies devised by an organization's senior management. In fact, the change process can often be slotted into the project-management structure of an organization if it already has such a structure in place.

The advantage of a project-management approach is that it gives you – the person responsible for seeing that the change happens – a way in which to have control over the change process. This control comes from your ability to check that everything that needs to be done is done (and at the right time). And you can make things easier for everyone involved by providing a common language that they can understand and a well-defined process that they can follow.

A Balanced Approach

Some changes are small, involving a minor transition that affects just a few people. Others are huge, impacting upon thousands of people scattered all over the world. Whatever the size of the change, the potential causes of resistance will be the same, as will the process that you have to follow to manage the change. But the way in which you structure that process will alter in proportion to the size of the change: the larger the project, the more structuring will be required and the greater the volume of necessary project plans, collected data, spread sheet analyses and reports there will be.

Gauging *exactly* how much work you need to do, how much data to collect, how many people to survey, and so on, are skills that you can acquire only through experience. This is where your judgment comes into play. You could start off by collecting the minimum amount of data you think you will need, and add to it later if necessary. For example, if you are confident that you can predict resistance accurately by getting together with some of the people impacted upon by the change and sketching it out on a napkin over lunch, that's fine – you achieve your result with an economy of time and effort. However, if you feel subsequently that you need to survey more people who will be affected by the change in order to get a more accurate picture, you can proceed to do this, knowing that the money spent on your initial, informal sounding has been minimal.

As the person responsible for implementing the change, you are the one who must remain in control of managing it. Following the change-management strategies presented in this book will give you *effective* control; when you can gauge accurately how much to do in each change project, you will have *smart* control.

WHO SHOULD MANAGE CHANGE?

In short, *you* should. If you manage people, whether it's two or 20,000, a key part of that responsibility is to make change happen. Why? Because neither you nor your business will survive if you stay the same. Improving processes and increasing the quality of your output, increasing the skill and ability of your staff, putting in new software systems to make things more efficient, and so on, are the only ways in which you and your operation will remain competitive.

Very often, you will be asked to initiate changes by the people to whom you report, whether that's the shareholders or the board of directors. In other cases, you may have the authority to make your own decision that change needs to happen. In either case, the people who work for you will regard you, in the language of change management, as a **sponsor**. This means that you are the one who sees to it that they, and your operation, change.

Whether you manage others or not, you may be assigned responsibility for planning and implementing change. This makes you a **change agent**. And if the changes are wide-reaching – for example, organization-wide or department-wide – you may be given a special assignment, which involves taking on the role of full-time change agent.

If changes directly affect you and you yourself have to change, you are also a **target** of the change: that is, a person who changes. So it is possible to be a sponsor, a change agent and a target simultaneously. Each of these roles has a specific function, unique responsibilities and a clear job description. We will discuss these roles in more detail in Chapter 3.

Putting a Governance Structure in Place

If the change you need to make will affect people across a number of operations within the organization, you need to think especially carefully about how you should organize two of these roles – the sponsor and the change agent.

Large-scale change requires teams of change agents and sponsors, not just individuals. These teams need to be assembled and given charters and job descriptions that clearly set out their roles early in the change project so that they can operate effectively to make the change successful. On the other hand, if your changes are small, you may not need to create large, formal teams. However, even if the sponsor, change agent and target of your change are just you, a single individual, you will need to take on the same responsibilities that in much larger changes would be carried out by teams.

If you have previous experience of working on a large change project that incorporated project management, you may already be familiar with the specific roles of the Steering Team and the Implementation Team. The Steering Team is comprised of sponsors who oversee the change, ensuring that the change fits in with the organizational vision as a whole and that individuals perform their sponsor roles. This team gives the change agents direction; it provides resources to ensure a successful change; and it holds the change agents accountable for accomplishing the changes on time and within budget.

The Implementation Team is made up of change agents who are responsible particularly for defining, planning and implementing the actions that result in change. Their responsibilities are to identify tasks; to determine the resource requirements; and to track key implementation issues through each phase.

For effective change, we advocate adding a third team: the Change Management Team. This consists of a special category of change agents who work for the Implementation Team. They identify what could cause resistance among the targets and provide the strategies to reduce that resistance. They ensure that the communication, learning and reward plans are properly structured and implemented. And they also ensure that the change agents address resistance, that the Steering Team and the Implementation Team perform effectively, and that all the sponsors and change agents know what they are expected to do.

WORK SOLUTION 2

Setting up your Governance Structure

Use this work solution to help you to define your "governance structure" – the people who will manage your organization through the change.

1. Select the members of the Steering Team. Determine the size of the team based on the scope of the change. Define that scope by finding all the people who will be impacted by the change – the targets. Invite a manager from each department that is a target group to join the Steering Team.

2. Select the members of the Implementation Team. Pick people with knowledge of the current operation, who have an understanding of what you are changing to, and skill and experience in effecting change. Make sure you don't select an individual simply because he or she is available.

3. Select the members of the Change Management Team. Obviously, here it would be good to include people who have previous experience of implementing change, or at least some knowledge of change management strategies.

4. Now develop team charters. Ask yourself what are the responsibilities and boundaries of each team? Where should the charters be displayed so that everyone affected by the change can read them? Should all the teams have copies of all the charters so that each understands what the others have to do? Who will each team report to and how often?

5. Finally, obtain approval from all the sponsors. Make sure that all the bosses of departments affected by the change agree with your governance structure.

chapter 2

CHANGE AS A PROCESS

If you have had experience of trying to introduce changes in your organization in the past, you may have seen people act in ways that made no sense to you. When you told them that there was going to be a change, they kept asking you about it. When you explained that the change was necessary, they kept challenging the need to do it. Perhaps, after a while, you became impatient with them. How could they *not* see the need to change? Why weren't they eagerly embracing the change?

The answer is that you probably underestimated people's requirement for information about the change. They need this information so that they can arrive at a rational and intelligent decision as to whether to support or to resist the plans that are afoot. So it makes sense to keep everyone well-informed about each step of the change process.

In this chapter we explore the answers to three vital questions that employees commonly ask: Why do we have to change? What are we changing to? and How are these changes going to happen?

STARTING WITH TODAY

Did you drive to work yesterday? If you drove, did you have to think about the route you took – which corner to turn at, whether to go right or left? Probably not. You know the way. You are comfortable with that way because it doesn't take a lot of effort. It may not be the best route to work, or the shortest, or the most efficient, or the fastest. But because it is so comfortable, you keep on using it.

The same applies in business. An organization is structured around core processes that operate to achieve an overall business strategy. The current state of the organization is the way things are now. The trouble is that the way things are now may be historical – retained long after they cease to be the most efficient or the fastest ways simply because no one has bothered to update them. Everyone may be aware that the current state isn't the best it could be. They just follow the established processes that they know and understand – they have no wish to disturb the status quo. It is only when, say, customers start to take away their business because of the organization's lack of efficiency (for example, when problems meeting delivery dates occur) that someone takes notice.

At some point – perhaps when the directors start complaining because profitability is shrinking and costs are going up – someone with enough authority to do something about it says, "Find out what's going wrong. Figure out what our situation is." Then the people who are assigned this job, the change agents, start to do an analysis of the way things are. They would find it helpful to look at the current state from the following four angles, which we will consider in turn.

1. Structure

Is the structure of the organization at the heart of the problem? For example, does the difficulty lie in the chain of command up through the organization – who reports to whom? Or is the structure too centralized (or decentralized)? The technology used by the organization is also part of its structure. Does the problem lie here? For example, has the telephone system kept pace with the organization's growing needs? Are the computers (and their software) outdated? Is other essential equipment, such as machine tools, constantly breaking down and affecting productivity levels?

2. Process

Is the way in which work flows through the organization efficient? Do bottlenecks occur anywhere and slow down the workflow? For example, if one item on a customer's order is out of stock, does it delay the delivery of the whole order?

3. People

Do people in the workforce currently have the competence, experience, skills and knowledge that they need in order to carry out their tasks properly?

4. Culture

Is the culture of the organization, the beliefs of the workers regarding the work, the customers and the business in general, detrimental to success? Do these beliefs cause people to behave in ways that hamper success?

A close analysis of the structure, processes, people and culture will tell you a lot about the current state of the organization. When you pass this information on to the employees it will make it much easier for the people who will be most affected by the change to understand *why* things need to change. Then they will also appreciate the possible consequences of not changing and the reasons why the current situation cannot be allowed to continue.

Changing the way in which people have operated for a long time is not straightforward. If you are able to give them a clear picture of where the problem lies and how bad it is, you will help them to make an informed decision as to whether to support the change or resist it. The work solution opposite will show you how to create that picture.

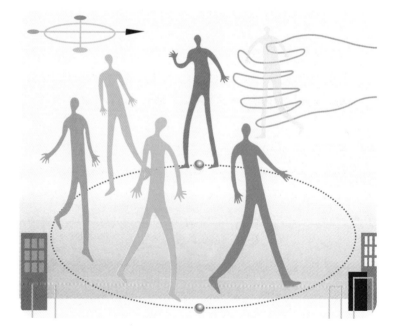

WORK SOLUTION 3

Creating the Picture

Before embarking upon any change, it is important to start with an accurate picture of how things stand today. This exercise will help you to answer the vital question: "Why are we changing – what's wrong with the current state?"

1. Take a pen and some paper. At the top of the page write "Current State." Now divide the page into four quarters and label them: Structure, Process, People and Culture.

2. First, analyze the structure of the organization. Ask yourself: Who reports to whom? What are the key roles and responsibilities? What systems and technology does the organization use? Write your answers under "Structure."

3. Next consider the process. Ask yourself how the work flows – from whom to whom and from where to where? Are there any barriers or duplications? Which processes are key to the organization? Put these answers under "Process."

4. Now look at your human resources. What kinds of skills do your employees possess? What types of knowledge do they have? What kinds of experience do they have? Jot down these answers under "People."

5. Finally, evaluate the culture. What are the organization's core values? What do employees believe is important? How do they behave? What kinds of rules, unwritten and written, do they follow? Write these answers under "Culture."

6. Keep this picture somewhere safe – you will need to refer to it again soon.

FINDING REASONS TO CHANGE

You have now built up a picture of the way the organization is today. But this alone is not enough – before you can implement change, you need to determine three other things: How do you know that something is wrong with the current state? What aspects of the current state cannot stay the same? How serious is the problem?

Usually the management already has some inkling of what is wrong. For example, people notice that customer complaints about poor service are increasing. Or they know that their technology is slow and out of date; or that a competitor just launched a major new product into the marketplace and their organization hasn't even sent its version into production yet.

However, that's not enough either. You need to know *by how much* complaints from customers have increased. And how does that figure compare with your competitors' experience? Or, given that your technology is slow, what are the implications? Do the resulting inefficiencies make your delivery slow? If so, how slow? The more quantifiable the data gathered by you, your management and the people who will have to change, the easier it will be to decide *what* to change.

However, even this amount of information is insufficient. The next step is to look at your analysis of the structure, process, people and culture (see p.37) to determine how one affects the others. (For example, the database is out of date, and knowing this leads the workers to believe that the data isn't necessary in the first place – an even greater problem.) The work solution opposite will show you how to do this.

WORK SOLUTION 4

Analyzing Why the Current State Has to Change

In Work Solution 3 (see p.39) you identified the current state of your organization. Using the information gathered then, complete this exercise to help you discover what is wrong with that picture and why it has to change.

1. Take a pen, some paper and the answers you gave in Work Solution 3. As you are reading each answer, ask yourself: Is this situation still acceptable? Mark any answers that are not.

2. Write one sentence describing *why* each unacceptable item is unacceptable. Add any hard evidence – for example, facts and figures to support your case. Then add any anecdotal evidence, such as stories and complaints from staff.

3. Now look for links between the problems. Is a problem in the People sector – say, a lack of skills – affecting one or more of the others? If so, write these links down. On a separate page note the ultimate impact on the organization's performance, such as loss of market share.

4. On another page answer the following questions: How much time do I have before the situation becomes more difficult and expensive to repair? Is the current situation caused by internal problems (which you can address) or external problems (which may be beyond your control)?

5. You now have your reasons to change. They form the basis of the argument you will present to the sponsor(s) to get the resources to make the change. They are also part of the information people need in order to change.

MOVING TOWARD TOMORROW

Now that you have a clear understanding of what needs to change in your organization, your next logical step is to determine how you wish things to change — to reach the desired state. So let's move on to the fun part of the change process — designing the future.

The desired state has the same four components as the current state: structure, processes, people and culture. In the current state each of these sectors is connected to the others, and a change in one is probably going to have an impact on the others. It's therefore true that no major change can occur by attending to just one, two or three of these components. Let us explain by example.

The Bloomerton Insurance Company has several problems in its organization. If we break them down into the four components of structure, process, people and culture, the current state of this organization looks as follows. Structure: at the moment there are seven layers of management, which makes reporting from the bottom to the top of the organization a lengthy procedure. Process: issuing policies requires multiple sign-offs and this slows down the whole procedure of taking out new policies. People: the sales staff who deal directly with customers only have knowledge of the type of policies they themselves sell, such as home and contents insurance, which prevents them from offering other products, such as building insurance, as add-on sales. Culture: there is a belief that risk-taking should be avoided, so the organization has been reluctant to move into new areas until these have been proven profitable by competitors.

Benchmarking against competitors, Bloomerton realizes it must make changes. Its aim is to improve the sale of new policies by at least 25 per cent and to become more innovative and competitive. To do this, Bloomerton decides to purchase the latest customer-relations management software, which will help them to find out the needs of customers and tailor the company's products to those needs. However, the new software alone cannot deliver the change. In order to derive the maximum benefit from the new technology and to achieve the 25 per cent increase in sales of new policies, other changes also have to be made at the same time.

Let's see where by looking again at the four components in turn. Structure: the organization must eliminate at least three layers of management to speed access up and down the organizational hierarchy. Process: the new software will give the sales staff the tools to enable them to analyze potential customers. So the approval procedures must change to reflect this new skill and give the sales personnel either the authority to select or reject customers on the spot, or more say in the customer-selection procedure. Both of these steps will speed up the issuing of new policies. People: sales personnel need more training and a better understanding of how the business runs so that they can obtain as much information from potential customers as possible during calls and sell more products. And finally, culture: the people who are given more authority must be willing to use it and to take responsibility for the decisions they make. In this way, the decision to increase sales so that Bloomerton can become more innovative and competitive has an effect on all four components of the desired state.

As with the current state, it is extremely important to set out your case for the desired state with as much documentary evidence, such as sales projections and potential savings, as you can. Documentation of the desired state gives the senior management the clear picture they need in order to approve the change and provide the necessary resources. Your documentary evidence also gives the change agents a clear understanding of the changes they are going to implement, and most importantly it gives the targets – the people who have to change – the information they need in order to understand how (and why) they are being asked to change.

Creating the desired state should be viewed as a "work in progress." It is a living organism that you need to review and revise periodically as new information becomes available

and greater detail is revealed. Both management and workers must understand that although the desired state that you have defined is the goal, it is not set in stone. As the world changes around you, your business must be ready to anticipate and react to those changes. And, therefore, at any time, you might have to modify the change accordingly.

WORK SOLUTION 5

Evaluating the Desired State

Using the decisions that you've already made about what to change, create a picture of the desired state. This will also help you to check whether you have included everything that needs to change and how your change might trigger other changes.

1. Take a pen and some paper. At the top of the page write "Desired State." Now divide the page into four quarters and label them: Structure, Process, People and Culture.

2. Using the analysis of the current state you did in Work Solutions 3 and 4, ask yourself: What would the four components look like if the problems in the current state were resolved? Write your answers in the appropriate quarters.

3. On a separate page, answer the following questions: What elements of the desired state (if any) are final and not negotiable? How long will it take to reach the desired state (see p.54)? (This will be important when devising the change schedule and allocating resources.) What could be open to adjustment, modification or elimination? (This will be important when people impacted by the change begin to negotiate with you about the things they don't want changed.) How will management know when the organization has reached the desired state? (This will be important in order to determine when to declare the change a success.) How stable will the desired state be? (This will be important when people try to modify the change once your project is over.)

4. Save this work. It contains useful information that will help you to review what has to evolve during the life-cycle of the change.

ALIGNING THE FUTURE WITH THE BUSINESS STRATEGY

Once you have mapped out the desired state that will "fix" the problems you identified in the current state, it is vital to check that the future you are planning aligns with your organization's overall business strategy.

If there is a written copy of this business strategy, you can use it to check that your desired state fits in with the broader organizational vision. If not, arrange a meeting with senior management to find out. The last thing you want to do is spend a great deal of time designing changes and implementing them only to discover that they conflict with your organization's plans. Having to rethink your desired state is a waste of time, money and effort. Also, if you don't check the alignment now and have to start again later, your implementation time will probably be shorter and more stressful.

Of course, your change also needs to fit in with any other major changes going on in your organization. Research what

else is changing – for example, by liaising with department managers – so that you can assess how any other changes might impact on or be impacted by your change. This may work to your advantage, if, say, you can pool resources with another department, or you discover a strategy that already proved successful elsewhere in the organization.

WORK SOLUTION 6

Checking the Alignment

Any change you make must fit within your organization's business strategy. Working through this exercise will help you check that the desired change is right for your organization.

1. Ask for an overview of the business strategy for your organization. Make sure you understand what the strategy means and the plans that the senior management have for achieving it. If you do not understand the plan, ask your sponsor to explain it to you.

2. Examine your desired state in relation to the overall business strategy. Does your change seem to contribute to that strategy? If not, refine your desired state so that it fits better with the business strategy.

3. Look at your change in relation to any other changes that are happening in or planned for your organization. Have a meeting with the change agents of those other changes and ask them to explain to you their desired states and how these contribute to the business strategy.

4. Now compare your desired state with the others. Is there any conflict between the change projects? If so, consult the other change agents and decide who needs to make modifications to bring all the changes into alignment.

5. Get in touch with the other change agents regularly to ensure that any modifications they have to make to their changes don't knock yours out of alignment with the organization's business strategy, and vice versa.

GAINING CONSENSUS

The picture of the desired state is like an idealized drawing of your dream house: door open wide and welcoming, smoke coming out of the chimney, and so on. Everyone agrees that this is a beautiful house. However, on closer inspection you realize that the house is painted light gray. While some of the family like gray, others wish it were light brown or white.

Likewise, the people with the authority and responsibility to decide that a change needs to be made often fail to agree on what the change needs to be because they do not look closely enough at the picture. Later, when the house is half painted, they squabble about the color, leaving you in the middle (or on the ladder holding the paint brush).

You have already taken steps to make sure that your desired state is aligned with the business strategy. Now, before going off to refine the picture of the desired state, and certainly before implementing the change, take time to ensure

that *all* the key managers who will have to support the change and live with the results have a clear idea of what the changed world will be like. Also check that they have reached consensus among themselves to support you in implementing the change. This isn't always easy, but the following Work Solution will show you how.

WORK SOLUTION 7

Obtaining Consensus on the Desired State

Everyone who is going to be affected by the change looks at it from their own perspective. That includes the management: those above you, those around you and, if you have them, managers who report to you. Use this exercise to find out what they all think of your proposed change.

1. Make a list of all the managers who are going to be impacted by the change, including people who are affected indirectly. For example, someone who simply receives reports from your department might need to be included because the information will henceforth be presented in a new way.

2. Arrange for these managers to review the desired state you have created. Such reviews can be done on a one-to-one basis or in group meetings.

3. Ask the managers whether the desired state makes sense to them. Can they support these changes within their own area of responsibility?

4. If there is disagreement over the desired state or an unwillingness to agree to support it, adjust and modify the desired state to satisfy them, if you can do so without compromising the change. If you can't adjust or modify the aim without compromising the change, explain why and note, for the record, who disagrees and how strong their feelings are.

5. If you have had several separate meetings and made several adjustments or modifications as a result of the meetings, get back to everyone you met with and let them know the outcome and any action you've taken subsequently.

WHAT'S IN IT FOR ME?

Your task is to make the organization more successful by making a change. Up to this point you have been looking at that change from an organizational perspective. You have got the management who have to support this change to review your desired state. However, within each department there is a structure, a process and a culture that potentially will be impacted by the change, as well as people who will be affected by it.

Everyone impacted by the change will first try to understand why the organization has to change and *then* ask the question, "What's in it for me?"

The answer to this question will help anyone affected by the change to assess whether they will accept or even welcome the change or resist it (regardless of whether or not it seems like a good idea for the organization as a whole).

Here are some of the most common questions that individuals affected by targets of change usually wish to know:

• Will I like the new way of doing things?

• What, if anything, will stay the same?

• Will I lose my job? If not, how will my job change?

• Will I have a different boss?

• Will I have the same colleagues?

• Are we moving to a new location?

• Can I keep my X (this could be anything from a favorite piece of equipment, such as a computer, to a special working arrangement, such as an agreement that the employee can do flexible hours)?

• If I can't work in the new way, what will happen to me?

It is important to arm yourself with answers to the above questions as early as possible in the change process. Keep telling people everything you know when you know it, and make it personal. For example: "Joachim, we don't know yet what department you will report to, but we do know that you will receive training on the computer in how to enter the new data."

If you don't have enough detail at an individual level to be able to give the targets all the information they desire, try at least to let them know *why* you don't have the answers now. Then, as soon as possible, tell them when you *will* be able to enlighten them.

ACCENTUATE THE POSITIVE

Keep in mind that everyone looks at change from their own perspective. This is why it is always good to try to find something positive to present to those affected, even if the desired state is still evolving.

If there are elements of the desired state that employees find undesirable, they are likely to resist the change. So, if you know that people are unhappy about the change, try to reassure them. For example, if someone is worried because their job is changing drastically, explain that they will learn a new skill or process that will enhance their career. Or, if they are wary of new technology, stress how the improved software will enable them to work faster.

If the change threatens someone's job, you can still turn the situation around by highlighting the positive aspects of the change. For example, their job in order processing may be disappearing, but they will be transferred to customer services. Even if they are going to lose their job altogether, you can lessen the blow by, say, stressing that they will be offered a generous redundancy package and/or support with finding a new position. If you look hard enough you can find something positive in almost any change situation.

THE DELTA STATE

Between where you are today – the current state – and where you will be tomorrow – the desired state – is the delta, the space where change happens. The delta state is not the old way of doing business; nor is it the new way. It is a time in between the two, when the transition from the current to the desired occurs.

We all react to the delta state in different ways. While some of us thrive on change, finding it challenging and energizing, others find it stressful and confusing. The key to making the delta a positive experience for those affected by change is to manage it well and offer them as much information and support as possible through the transition period.

Let's first examine why people find the delta state so stressful, before we go on to suggest ways in which to improve their transition experience. Stress and insecurity in the delta state can come from many sources. People may be stressed because they are expected to do their regular job *and* learn to do the new job at the same time. Or they may be sad because they are leaving colleagues and/or moving to a new location. Or, they may be apprehensive because they have not been told enough about what happens next in the process of change. Ultimately, if the difficulties of the delta state become too much for people, they may reject the desired state and go back to the old and comfortable way of doing things simply because they know what to expect there.

So how can you make the delta state a better experience for all concerned? First, you need to show them that you have a plan to help them get from the current to the desired

state. If they know that you are creating a step-by-step plan to guide them through the transition, making available all the tools, resources and support they will need, this will give them confidence and reassurance. Second, acknowledge their fears, stress and discomfort. Assure them that their confusion is legitimate and encourage them to ask you questions to help clarify things for them. Make sure you answer these questions. Third, encourage people to build their own skills to deal with the transition. Explain clearly their roles, the role of management and the reasons why change can cause difficulties, and urge them to be more proactive in seeking any information and support they need to reduce their anxieties.

DETERMINING THE SPEED OF CHANGE

One of the biggest problems with the delta state is that people perceive it as being either too short ("This is happening at the speed of light") or too long ("They will be implementing this thing until the next century"). If people think things are happening too fast, they resent being "pushed" and may resist the change. Conversely, if they feel that the change is dragging along, they begin to lose the point of learning new procedures and would rather be left to get on with their regular work. The key word here is "perceive." What is the reality? *Is* the change happening too fast or too slow? How fast should the change happen, and why?

The length of time you will need for the delta is determined by the information you gathered about what is wrong with the current state. Next you need to ask: How long do you have before *not* changing threatens your organization? The answer to this question sets the parameters for the change. Start by breaking down the change into key stages and assessing how long each one will take. Then devise a calendar for the implementation and explain what has to happen when and why. Try to adhere rigorously to the change calendar you create so that you make living in the delta state less pressurized for everyone involved in the change.

Always schedule more time than you estimate you will need, to allow for contingencies. Even if you have plenty of time, minimize the transition period in which people have to juggle their regular work with the new work. Everyone will appreciate your careful planning and regard for their welfare and so be more willing to cooperate during this period.

THE CHANGE CALENDAR

A change calendar is not just a timeline of when your change starts and finishes, it is much more. On pp.24–5 we listed the questions that you need to answer in order to achieve a well-managed change. The answers to these questions provide logical steps that form the basic plan of action or milestones for your change. Now all you have to do is add a schedule for each step and you will have an easy-to-follow change calendar.

Pin up your calendar somewhere where all those concerned can see it. This will enable them to find out what has to be done and by when, and also what has been accomplished so far. Displaying your change calendar in this way will tell people something else, too – that you have planned the change well and have it under control.

To create your own change calendar, first determine the start-to-finish time-frame by answering the following questions. What is the longest delta state the organization can tolerate? What happens if the change takes longer than that? Could the change be implemented even faster than that?

Now create a grid like the one below. We have shown four action steps (but you can add as many as you need) and we have filled in the first row only to give an example of the achievements you might wish to display. Write in the start date and the date by which you need to complete each action step. Next, determine the intervals of time to be used as milestones (weeks, as in our example, or months or quarters). Then, down the left-hand side, fill in the action steps as appropriate.

ACTION STEP	START DATE	Week 1	Week 2	Week 3	Week 4	END DATE
Determine the Case for Change	June 5	Data gathered	Data analyzed	Findings presented to sponsors	Case for change greenlit	July 6
Design the Desired State						
Create the Master Action Plan						
Identify the Key Players						

THE DIP IN THE DELTA

As the change proceeds the delta state can become difficult, even chaotic. The workload increases as staff try to keep the organization running the "old way" while struggling to learn and use the "new way." Meanwhile, senior management needs the change to be transparent to the customer.

Change seldom occurs without some negative impact on the organization during the delta state. For example, productivity may dip while people take time out from their day-to-day responsibilities to attend training. Or, staff might spend time speculating about the desired state or complaining about the changes, resulting in reduced productivity.

This negative impact on the day-to-day running of the organization is what we call the "dip in the delta." An organization can't afford to suffer too much of a dip or customers might start to take their business elsewhere, investors start to sell the stock, and so on. This is why it is vital to consider issues such as: How much productivity can you sacrifice during the next six months while you install the new system? Or, how much of a sacrifice can you afford in levels of customer services, or other aspects of the business, while your staff learn their new roles?

Implementing a change and keeping the organization going may seem directly in opposition to each other, so how should you proceed? First, as a change agent, it is your job to predict how bad the dip might be. Ask yourself what could go wrong and what is the probability that such things will happen. How are targets likely to behave through the delta state? What is the impact of their behavior likely to be on the day-to-day running of the organization? Then, identify the danger threshold. Where does the dip become intolerable for the organization to absorb? What are the core functions of the organization? Ask yourself and management above you how much of a reduction in these functions the organization could withstand before serious damage occurred.

By managing the change well and by reducing resistance, you will go a long way toward leveling the dip in the delta. However, if these measures prove inadequate you can further reduce the dip by modifying your desired state to keep a balance between implementing the change and sustaining the organization's core functions at an acceptable level.

MAKING IT THROUGH THE DIP

You are trying your best to make going through the change as positive an experience as possible for everyone involved. However, despite all your efforts, many people are finding it hard to cope with the dip in the delta. What can you do to help them?

First, respect and acknowledge the difficulty that some of the employees are experiencing. Let people know that you understand how hard it is to learn a new technique or a new process. Give them an example of something that you, personally, are finding tough so that they realize they are not alone. Let them know that you realize how stressful it is to come to work each day wondering if this is the day when the change is going to "bite."

On a practical level, do everything you can to reduce people's stress levels. You could lighten workloads temporarily; or give staff time off; or if this is not possible, let them take, say, an extra 15 minutes for lunch. Another idea would be to arrange for a masseur to come in one day a week to give everyone a neck massage. Or you could bring back a trusted, retired worker to counsel people and offer them support.

Showing that you care may take time, effort and a little money, but it will be worth it to help staff make it through the dip.

LIVING IN THE DELTA STATE

A word about coming to terms with the delta state – it's a good idea to try to get used to it! One of the greatest benefits of effective change management is that it teaches people how to live in a state of constant change. Adapting to the point where you become comfortable in a constantly changing environment is a key competitive advantage for your organization. If your organization can tolerate a greater amount of change than your competitors, you have the advantage. Your rivals have to make the same choices as you do about *what* to change. They read the same books, hire the same consultants, and listen to the same vendors or customers. It is in *how* you implement change that your organization can gain the cutting edge.

This means that everyone who works for your organization, from the chief executive downward, must get used to living in a constant state of ambiguity. And that you, as a change agent (and/or a sponsor and/or a target), must play your part in developing the mechanisms that will help your staff to live in that environment.

The delta state often involves temporary compromises – for example, workers sharing facilities, or making do with old equipment to start new tasks. As a change agent, it's important that you take an interest in the temporary conditions under which people are working. Show that you too are prepared to accept compromises – anything from offering to help move furniture to lending your laptop. Always ask if you can help – it's unlikely that anyone will press you to do something that goes against yours or the organization's interests.

The Positive Sides of Change

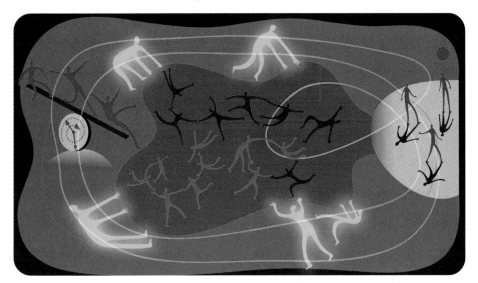

When the delta state becomes too difficult for you, or for one of the targets, to take philosophically any more, it's worth reminding yourself or them of its positive advantages:

• It enables everyone in the department or organization to work together cohesively toward a common purpose.

• It's the logical next step in the organization's organic life – and so it's one step nearer to the desired state.

• It prevents the organization from becoming fossilized in old and outmoded practices.

• It gives staff the chance to learn new skills and new roles.

• It gives everyone the opportunity to show their commitment to common goals.

• It shows outsiders that the organization is highly responsive to the conditions in which it operating – for example, the economic climate and advances in technology.

chapter 3

ROLES AND RESPONSIBILITIES

In the past few years there has been much discussion in business circles about leadership. And one of the key topics of every discussion is change. After all, leaders do not achieve success by maintaining the current state. By definition, their job is to change the status quo and make progress.

It is therefore most appropriate to examine the role and responsibilities of the change leaders (the sponsors) who authorize and provide the resources for change. However, of equal importance are the people who have to deliver the change – the change agents. Their skills in implementing the project, and in gaining the support of those who have to change (often termed the "targets"), make a powerful contribution to its success. Likewise, the targets themselves have their own vital part to play, because without their cooperation there can be no change.

In this chapter we explore in depth the roles and responsibilities of each of these key players. We learn how to assess how well each one is fulfilling their role and what steps we can take to overcome resistance and improve performance.

Earlier, on pp.30–31, when we talked about setting up a structure for the change, we defined three key roles: the sponsor, the change agent and the target. Let's take a closer look at these roles, the responsibilities that go with each of

them, and the relationships these people have to each other. In addition, we will explore another label used by many organizations: the stakeholder.

Your organization may already use these titles – or others, such as "partner in change" rather than "target." These terms are important because titles are powerful. But their meanings are even more important. We have found that labels often have fuzzy or overlapping definitions. This means that people sometimes become confused about what they are expected to do and who is supposed to do what.

Let's start then with a recap of the labels we use and their definitions. (You can adjust the labels to fit your organization, but make sure that whatever label you use for each of these roles has an accompanying clear and well-articulated job description. Ensure that everyone understands those roles and the differences between them.)

First we have the sponsor, or sponsors. These are usually senior managers or leaders within the organization, who have the authority to decide that something should change and to allocate resources to support that change.

THE KEY ROLE MAP

Before you embark on a change, it is important to know who the key players will be. A good way to identify them is to build up a picture of who has which role(s) – in other words, a Key Role Map.

At first glance the map may resemble an organization chart – a diagram that shows the structure of an organization. However, the Key Role Map is more versatile because it also identifies who plays which roles. By giving information about each level of the workforce, The Key Role Map identifies the sponsors, the change agents and the targets. It also highlights who plays multiple roles.

The Key Role Map can be used as a tool for assessment. For example, you can use the map to pinpoint sponsors, change agents and targets who are causing problems by not fulfilling their roles in the change.

However, you can also use the map as a tool for communication, as it allows targets to see who the sponsors and change agents are. Placing a Key Role Map on a noticeboard where everyone can see it is a valuable way to show the targets that you want them to understand and support the change. Naturally, if you use the map to communicate you will need to ensure that it contains no potentially sensitive assessments of people. Step-by-step guidance on creating and using your own Key Role Map is given on p.65.

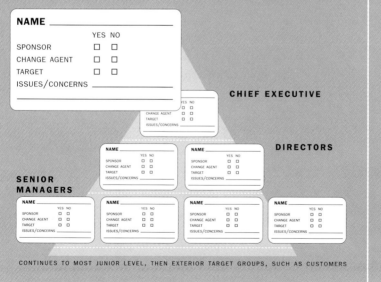

	YES	NO
SPONSOR	☐	☐
CHANGE AGENT	☐	☐
TARGET	☐	☐

CHIEF EXECUTIVE

DIRECTORS

SENIOR MANAGERS

CONTINUES TO MOST JUNIOR LEVEL, THEN EXTERIOR TARGET GROUPS, SUCH AS CUSTOMERS

Second, we have the change agents. These are people within the organization who are assigned the task of planning and implementing the change by the sponsors. Change agents can be sponsors too.

Third, we have the targets, the people who have to change. We realize that "target" is a very strong word. For this reason many sponsors and change agents suggest that we soften this label or change it to "partners in the change process." We prefer to keep the word "target" for a good reason. You have only to ask the people who are impacted by the change whether they feel they are a "target" or a "partner," and in our experience most say "target." Sometimes a target can also be a sponsor and a change agent.

Last, we come to the new label of stakeholder – the term given to everyone affected by the change, including all sponsors, change agents, targets and, sometimes, bystanders. Occasionally it may be used as a substitute word for "target."

Each of these roles is dependent on the others. If the sponsors do not make the decision to change or provide the resources needed for change, the change agents do not have a change to work on and the targets are the targets of nothing. If the change agents do not plan and manage the change there is a risk that the change will not happen and that the efforts of the sponsors and the targets will go to waste. Similarly, if the targets do not change, the work of the sponsors and change agents will be in vain. Therefore, you must agree upon and define at the outset the labels, the responsibilities and the actions that go with each role.

WORK SOLUTION 8

Creating and Using Your Own Key Role Map

Your Key Role Map will be an invaluable guide to who plays which role(s) within your organization. This exercise shows you some possible ways to set up the map, as well as how to use it.

1. Turn to the Key Role Map chart on p.63. The idea is to create on paper a pyramid that reflects the structure of your organization, including everyone involved in the change with a note on their specific roles.

2. If you wish to identify individuals in your map, see if you can fit the templates shown onto a single large sheet of paper. If not, try using an index card for each person and write a numerical code at the top of each card. Then key these numbers into a simplified version of the pyramid that gives job titles and code numbers but no other details. The index cards can then be filed in a box.

3. In a large organization you might choose to have one Key Role Map for each department and a separate map to show how the departments relate to each other within the organization. In the latter case, of course, you might need to abandon the pyramid shape to reflect a less hierarchical structure.

4. Decide whether the Key Role Map is for for use by only yourself and your peers within the organization or for public display. If the latter, be sure that any comments you put under "issues/concerns" will not be a breach of confidence. Or, you could create one Key Role Map for assessment purposes and another for communication – one for private and one for public consumption.

CHANGE ADVOCATES

So far, we have been writing about a change scenario in which the sponsor decides what has to change and then exercises his or her authority to make it happen, and appoints the change agent. But you might be wondering where the idea for this change came from in the first place. In many cases, directors or senior management are the source of the initiative. However, these are not the only people in the organization who can come up with good ideas. Anyone can. It's just that when a great idea for change comes from someone without the authority to make it happen, it remains just that – a good idea. The inspired person can't be the sponsor

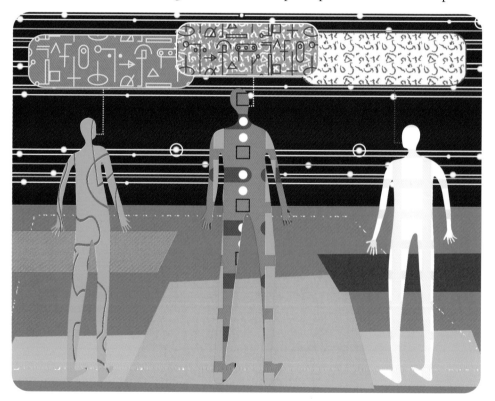

because he or she does not have the authority to make the change happen. Nor can they be a change agent, because no one with sufficient authority has given them the go-ahead. So the person who has the idea, but doesn't have the authority to implement it, is called something else entirely – a "change advocate."

Clearly, if you are a change advocate, your first step is to find a sponsor who can appoint someone (preferably you) to be the change agent and provide the resources and the support to make the change actually happen. Let's imagine that you are a change advocate who wishes to become a change agent. How would you go about finding a sponsor?

You should start by creating a Key Role Map (see pp.63 and 65) to identify who would be the most appropriate sponsor for this change. Pinpoint all the targets of your proposed change and work upward through the organization's hierarchy. If your path requires working up through multiple layers in the organization, you may need help from your own boss and someone above them to get to the potential sponsor. This means that when you present the change idea to your boss it's important to make them understand that you need them not only to buy into the change, but also to help present the case for change to their own boss – and so on, until you reach the natural sponsor.

Once you find the appropriate sponsor you will graduate from being a change advocate with a good idea to a change agent with the authority and resources to facilitate and implement that good idea and make the change happen.

THE SPONSOR

The first thing sponsors need to know is that they cannot authorize a change, appoint a change agent … and then walk away. Sponsors are often busy directors and senior managers. They run the business on a day-to-day basis, but they are also responsible for taking an active role in the many changes that frequently come across their desk. Sometimes they need reminding that their role in a change goes beyond merely authorizing someone else to make the change happen.

The responsibilities of the sponsor are threefold. A sponsor must understand the change; manage or oversee the change; and deal with the people affected by the change.

Let's follow an example through the three responsibilities. First, in order to understand the change as a whole, the sponsor must understand the desired state and the impact it will have on the workforce. Take the case of Jim Starr, the vice-president of Information Systems. Jim challenged the divisional managers who reported directly to him to cut costs. Research proved that the most effective way to do so was to make redundant long-serving, highly-paid computer programmers and outsource their jobs. But Jim felt that dismissing the workforce in order to cut costs was a negative solution. So he asked the change agents (the divisional managers) to devise an alternative plan. They proposed instead that economies be made by cutting the budgets for equipment, such as copiers and printers, within their departments. Jim found this a better solution – a change he could support.

The sponsor's second responsibility is to manage or oversee the change. However, terms such as "oversee" should be

used with caution as there is a danger that the role will be regarded as discretionary, or in some way not fully engaged with the practicalities of the change. In some cases the sponsor will agree with the change agent not to get involved in the day-to-day management of the change, whereas in other situations they might adopt a more hands-on, *managerial* role.

Even the manager who in a predetermined way oversees or presides over the change will need to have close contact at times with the targets. In our experience, targets of change like to deal directly with the sponsors. They don't want to hear about the why or the what or the how from change agents, who are seen as being at one remove from the source. A speech may by written by the change agents who know what questions the targets want the sponsors to address. The training may be designed and delivered by one or more of

the change agents. But the sponsors need to be there at the kick-off and to thank everyone at the end of the training. Who needs what reward is worked out by the change agents, but it should be the sponsor who congratulates the workers on their efforts.

Back with Jim at Information Systems, the change agents found that the analysts and programmers in IT were not too happy about the proposed economies in their department. They told Jim about this resistance and on their recommendation he took two main actions. First, he commissioned a video showing the state of IT in the organization and the need for change, and broadcast it on the intranet. Jim talked about what they would look like when they were "lean and mean" and asked for everyone's cooperation in doing an analysis of working practices.

The third task of a sponsor is to deal with the people affected by the change. Staff need to see the face of the person who is asking them to change. They need to see sincerity, understanding, support and encouragement behind the picture of the desired state. So next, Jim conducted a "speaking tour" around the IT division, using his speeches as an opportunity to praise those who had done the working-practice analysis. One of the stops on his tour was in the department where the long-serving, highly-paid computer programmers were based. When Jim began to talk about the need to lower costs in Information Systems, palms began to sweat until he said, "No one in this room will lose their job as a result of this change." The tension dissipated instantly. Jim

ASSESSING YOUR SPONSOR

Look at your Key Role Map (see p.63) and select a specific sponsor for assessment. Taking a pen and paper, write their name at the top of the page. Then, draw 3 columns with 6 rows across them to make a table consisting of 18 cells.

Fill in the 3 column headings and complete the left column of cells as shown in the example below. In the middle column write a summary of your sponsor's current position regarding fulfilling each responsibility and in the right hand column add a "gap rating." This is the gap between the current level of responsibility they have assumed and the level you would like them to take. Use the scale of 1 to 10, i.e. 1=small gap and 10=huge gap. If you have a sponsor whose performance is far from ideal, extend the assessment by asking yourself why there is such a gap between their actual and optimum performance. (For more on the reluctant sponsor, see pp.74–5.)

NAME OF SPONSOR: BOB STAPLETON

SPONSOR RESPONSIBILITIES	CURRENT POSITION	GAP RATING
To understand the shortfalls of the current state.	Has a good grasp of why change is necessary.	2
To agree on the definition of the desired state.	Has delegated this responsibility to the change agents.	3
To agree on the changes required in order to achieve the desired state.	Has agreed in principle.	2
To manage or oversee the change.	Has cleared space in workload to allow for change responsibilities.	4
To deal with the people affected by the change.	Is making himself available to listen to his staff's concerns.	3

earned great respect as a leader who communicated the desired state in terms that the workers understood. But the real advantage Jim gained by his face-to-face meetings with staff was the opportunity to exhibit his willingness to listen and to react directly to their fears about the change.

It is vital that sponsors carry out specific activities, such as those undertaken by Jim, to overcome resistance in targets. If sponsors are not able to fulfil their responsibilities, or if they choose not to fulfil them, the targets are more likely to resent and, ultimately, resist the change, which might put the whole change in jeopardy. To gauge the performance of your sponsor, try the assessment on p.71.

Your success as a change agent is highly dependent upon the ability and willingness of the sponsor to manage the targets, and you have a right to expect management to perform their assigned roles. However, if the sponsor shows any signs of uncertainty, or any reluctance, do not rush to judge them. Try to appreciate that, while they have been involved in changes at some point in their career, it is possible that they have never seen or experienced a change that was managed well. If lack of experience in effective change management is indeed the problem, you will need to adjust your expectations and guide the sponsor toward accepting and carrying out their responsibilities. More specific advice on dealing with the "reluctant sponsor" is given on pp.74–5.

WORK SOLUTION 9

Engaging Your Sponsor

Deciding what you need to make the change successful may be simple; but explaining those needs to your sponsor and getting him or her to agree to meet them may be more of a challenge. Use this exercise to help you.

1. Determine what resources and supportive action you need from your sponsor during both the planning and implementation steps. (This is tantamount to a sponsor's job description.) Write down these needs in a simple, easy-to-understand format.

2. Make an appointment with your sponsor. Provide this summary for them to review. Explain that this is the action needed to make the change project a success – that these are not your requirements, but the requirements of the change throughout the delta state.

3. Negotiate the degree to which and the frequency with which your sponsor will provide the suggested input. (In other words, ideally they should do everything you have detailed, but how much and how often is open for discussion.)

4. Set up a schedule for periodic reviews of the sponsor's input. For example, it might take one hour-long meeting per week with your sponsor to ensure that they are fully engaged in the change project. Or it might take more or less than this. Agree to the frequency and style of communication (for example, face to face, by email, and so on) you will use to stay in contact throughout the change process.

THE RELUCTANT SPONSOR

If your sponsor seems reluctant to cooperate, the first thing you have to do is figure out why. In our experience, it is usually for one of three reasons: the sponsor does not agree with the proposed change; the sponsor agrees with the change but they do not have the resources that the change requires; or the sponsor agrees with the change, but they do not have the time required to support it properly.

1. *The sponsor does not agree with the proposed change.*
To put it bluntly, if the sponsor disagrees with the change, the people who report to him or her have no change to manage.

The sponsor may have been pressured into supporting the change in the first place and is only now showing their true colors; or may have come to a revised view after learning what the change will involve; or new facts or opinions may have come to light about the background to the change, causing a change of heart.

To win over this type of reluctant sponsor you will need to equip yourself with all the key data about the current state and the desired state, including the reasons for change. The sponsor may not admit to having reservations about the change – and if so, nothing will be gained by forcing their hand. Better to build up a persuasive picture that carries the sponsor along on a tide of well-informed enthusiasm.

2. *The sponsor agrees with the change but does not have the resources that the change requires.*
Here, if the problem is lack of staff, you will have to either justify the expense of recruitment or show how existing staff within the organization can be reshuffled to fill the roles

available. At the same time you will need to analyze the consequences of *not* activating the change: fully spelled out, the prospect of these consequences will often prove conclusive. At least it will give you a scenario to weigh carefully with your reluctant sponsor against the change scenario.

3. The sponsor agrees with the change, but does not have enough time to support it properly.

Sometimes even the most senior people within an organization will work reactively on management issues – for example, problem-solving only when a problem is brought to their attention. If you detect a lack of initiative on the part of the sponsor, be neither defeatist nor confrontational. Instead, try

to appreciate the pressures upon the sponsor. To get them to give full commitment to the change, use persuasion, not criticism. Patiently set out your views, offering information you feel may be illuminating, as well as concrete help. Make it clear that you are aware of the many claims upon their time – then say why you believe that the change should be prioritized. To get the sponsor to do their job properly is part of *your* job as change agent.

THE CHANGE AGENT

Conflicting management goals, problematic staff, tight project deadlines, limited resources, and so on … Does this all sound familiar? Our guess is that you have already experienced some of these stressful aspects of working life, which also go with the territory of being a change agent.

Think about your position as a change agent logistically for a moment. In the hierarchy of the change there is a sponsor who is above you. Below you (and sometimes on either side of you) are the targets. Sounds like a sandwich! However, the real issue is that the people in each of these positions want something different from you. The sponsor is asking you to understand at a strategic level how the change will change the business and make it better. They speak in broad business terms and expect you to deliver the change fast and cost-efficiently. On the other hand the targets need you to explain all about the change in a way they can understand, and they also want you to tell them what makes the change worthwhile for them. And while you are contending with the different demands of the sponsor and targets, you are also trying to get your own regular work done! There's no doubt about it, being a change agent can be a tough job.

When you start out as a change agent, make sure that you have a clear idea of your responsibilities (and those of the other change agents, if applicable). Also, agree on performance criteria for your role with your sponsor. That way, you both know what is expected of you.

The change agent does not make the decision to change, nor allocate resources to the change, and in this sense does not "own" the change. The change belongs to the sponsor and to the people who are going to change. The change agent's job is to plan and implement the change on their behalf.

This is often hard for the change agent to remember. As a change agent you live and breathe the work of the change, and this can sometimes foster a proprietorial attitude. For example, when the targets do not quite conform to your calculations, or a small group of them derails one of your initiatives by raising perfectly valid objections or pointing out a flaw you hadn't noticed, you might feel yourself becoming resentful. You must resist such a tendency to identify emotionally with the change, because it is likely to make you inflexible. Remain engaged yet objective. An appropriate level of engagement involves detachment – and excludes passionate partisanship.

We have already mentioned here that sometimes the roles of sponsor and change agent are carried out by the same person. While at first this might seem problematic, the two roles are clearly different. If you are performing both roles, study them carefully and be aware of when to put your change-agent hat on and, as it were, write the speech, and when to put your sponsor hat on and deliver it. (See pp.68–73 for a detailed outline of the sponsor's role and responsibilities, and pp.92–3 for more on multiple roles.)

If there's one essential quality the change agent needs, it's the ability to listen. Then you can translate the needs expressed by the targets into actions that make the change easier for them to live through. Like the sponsor, you will need to understand the change thoroughly and relate well to all the people involved. However, the sponsor's exposure to the targets will probably be more limited than yours will be: you will have hours of contact with those involved in the change, and you will learn a great deal about them in the process. You will also be required, of course, to be highly efficient in your management of the change – that is, to put all your discoveries and calculations into practice, in the most cost-effective way possible and with the least damage in human terms.

After you have grasped the fundamental nature of the change, and the thinking behind it, you must ensure that the change is clearly defined in terms of structure, process, people and culture. You will need to understand how changing one feature of the organization will certainly impact upon another feature, and that in turn will impact upon a third; and that structural changes will in turn affect processes and people, in chain reactions. For example, imagine that two departments are being amalgamated and a third, small department is being created from the surplus staff thereby released to

ASSESSING THE CHANGE AGENT

Look at your Key Role Map (see p.63) and select a specific change agent for assessment. Taking a pen and paper, write their name at the top of the page. Then, draw 3 columns and 6 rows across them to make a table consisting of 18 cells.

Fill in the 3 column headings and complete the left column of cells as shown in the example below. In the middle column write a summary of your change agent's current position regarding fulfilling each responsibility and in the right hand column add a "gap rating." This is the gap between the current level of responsibility they have assumed and the level you would like them to take. Use the scale of 1 to 10, i.e. 1=small gap and 10=huge gap. Do this assessment for as many of the change agents on your Key Role Map as is practical and get them to assess you too. Agree how to address any areas of weakness and suggest ways in which you can each improve your performance.

NAME OF CHANGE AGENT: ROSITA FERNANDEZ

CHANGE AGENT RESPONSIBILITIES	CURRENT POSITION	GAP RATING
To understand the shortfalls of the current state.	Realizes why change is necessary.	2
To understand the definition of the desired state.	Has understood and accepted brief by sponsor.	1
To identify and measure the impact of the change on the structure, processes, people and culture.	So far has only determined impact on structure and process.	5
To determine the level and type of sponsorship required.	Has good knowledge of senior managers and access to top level.	2
To deal with the people affected by the change.	Has done initial assessment of target reactions.	3

carry out a completely new role within the organization – for example, in a large advertising agency these people might be diverted from their current jobs to establish a "new media" department, concerned with plasma screen advertising and the like. As soon as you start to think about making the structural change of shrinking two departments and creating one new department, you have to work out the new reporting lines. Who will run the new department? And if one of the two senior managers is moved to head the new media department, who will be in charge of the department from which they have been moved? There will often be difficult choices to make in terms of staffing: can one manager run two departments, or should a third person be promoted to senior managerial level? And in deciding which way to proceed, you will need to consider the individuals – their personalities, ambitions, abilities and potential. For although it is possible to design organizational change in terms of an idealized model, in the real world you have to deal with the people you have available. Some, of course, will be square pegs, and you will need to decide which round hole will be least uncomfortable for them.

To complicate the picture further, some of the ad agency's clients may need plasma screen products alongside their more traditional campaigns in print, screen and on-line media, so you will need to consider how the new department relates to the client base without unnecessary duplication of relationships. But then nobody ever said a change agent's role was going to be simple!

THE UNWILLING CHANGE AGENT

In large organizations, or if the change is a major one, it is sometimes necessary for a number of change agents to work together in a team or teams (see pp.30–33) The change team leader(s) will then be required to manage their change agents as well as to manage the targets. If appointed to this role, you will often be managing team members who have different degrees of skills and knowledge about how to make change happen. Some of the team members may even be unwilling change agents, wishing that they were not so closely involved in the change, or that their role were a less active one; others may be unable or reluctant to work as part of a team. To overcome these challenges will probably make considerable demands upon your people skills.

Once appointed to head the team, your first step should be to get to know the team and their attitudes to the change. It's sometimes a good idea to strengthen team bonds over a brown-bag lunch, or a meeting in the staff cafeteria, or even to arrange a semi-social occasion, perhaps in a rented room with refreshments provided. Try to draw out the most positive ingredients from the chemistry of the team. For example, you might find that someone has a talent for metaphor, and this can be harnessed in persuasive speechwriting. If someone has a confident authoritative-sounding voice that inspires trust in listeners, they might become the spokesperson and deliver some of these speeches – although you must be sure that the sponsor also talks to the staff. Anyone on the team who is knowledgeable about psychology might be able to help in talking matters through with emotionally-resistant targets – including other change agents.

Avoid the pitfall of allocating specific roles before you have spoken to the team members at length – some people may have strengths that their regular job descriptions disguise and others, by the same token, may have surprising blind spots.

It can be difficult to deal with the change agent who is reluctant to be part of the change. They may simply resent the fact that they have had change management added to their regular job responsibilities, or they may feel in some way threatened by the change. You may not be able to help to solve the unwilling change agent's problems, but you can help them to analyze what lies at the heart of their troubles, and then determine what is required to deal with the situation. Sometimes change team leaders encounter skepticism or, worse, cynicism: the best way to deal with these attitudes is to remain positive and optimistic, to show by your interactions that you value a constructive approach, and above all never to counter sarcasm with sarcasm.

THE TARGETS

Who are the targets? A target is anyone who has to change. Often we think of targets as a relatively small group of people on whom the change will have the biggest impact, and we stop there. When you did the Key Role Map and labeled the targets, you had to think beyond your own organization. Remember that targets can include people outside your organization, such as your customers. Each target has the potential to resist, and this resistance will come from their own perspective of the change.

So what *is* the targets' perspective? Often it is the perspective of the victim – someone to whom bad things are happening. If there is a victim mentality among the targets of your change, a key question is: How did they get that way? Did they come to work in your organization with that viewpoint, did they become like that for some reason after joining you, or did they learn to think that way because of the way they were treated in the organization's previous changes?

Targets have the right to complain when they simply have a change imposed on them without their participation. However, if the sponsor and change agent adopt a positive attitude toward targets and try to involve them in the change, complaints are less likely to occur.

Targets, like sponsors and change agents, need to understand the change, and to deal effectively with the other people involved – their fellow targets and their managers. Like change agents, the targets also need to manage the change –

ASSESSING TARGETS

Look at your Key Role Map (see p.63) and select a specific target (or target group) for assessment. Taking a pen and paper, write their name at the top of the page. Then, draw 3 columns and 6 rows across them to make a table consisting of 18 cells.

Fill in the 3 column headings and complete the left column of cells as shown in the example below. In the middle column write a summary of your target's or target group's current position regarding fulfilling each responsibility and in the right hand column add a "gap rating." This is the gap between the current level of responsibility they have assumed and the level you would like them to take. Use the scale of 1 to 10, i.e. 1=small gap and 10=huge gap. Now consider how to close the gap between the targets' current and desirable behaviour. Do they realize what is expected of them? If not, explain how you need them to fulfil their responsibilities in order for the change to be successful.

NAME OF TARGET GROUP: FINANCE DEPARTMENT

TARGET RESPONSIBILITIES	CURRENT POSITION	GAP RATING
To seek any additional information needed to fully understand the reason for the change.	Have requested further information on specific aspects of the reason for change.	2
To share any negative feedback about the change with the change agent and sponsors.	Have expressed some initial concerns.	3
To tolerate the upheavals of the delta state.	Are currently nervous about the degree of possible disruption.	5
To work with sponsors and change agents, not against them.	Clearly demonstrate a willingness to cooperate.	3
To make up their own mind(s) whether to support or resist the change.	At this stage seem likely to be supportive (but need reassurance).	4

inwardly and outwardly. They need to deal with its implications at a personal level and, having come to terms with those, they need to act constructively to make the change go as smoothly and painlessly as possible for everyone involved, including themselves.

Sometimes, of course, the shock of the proposed changes leaves targets hampered by an emotional residue. Perhaps they are fearful of losing privileges. They might have thought that their department was pulling its weight within the organizational structure, but now they learn – or they might read the situation this way – that its contribution was under par. Sometimes they might even feel guilty: perhaps they weren't working hard enough, or efficiently enough.

The targets can manage the change by overcoming such feelings. They can share their confusion or anger with the change agent and sponsor, not just with other targets. They can opt to commit to the change (to do this they don't have to be comfortable with all its aspects, they just need to look for the value and logic of the change). They can work to help to define the precise nature of the desired state. They can be tolerant of the upheavals of the delta state, accepting them as a natural part of change. And finally, they can help to maintain the stability of the desired state, once reached, by not slipping back into old ways.

The job description of the target calls for them to be productive and pro-active – even to the point of volunteering their energies. If they are able to fulfil these requirements, they earn the new title, "partner in the change process."

TARGET PRACTICE

You may have reservations with our use of the word "target." We agree that it is not a positive word. When we are asked why we don't substitute the words "change partner" or "change recipient," our response is to tell the following story – a true account of an incident that happened to us some years ago.

One of our consultants was in the boardroom of a large bank in New York City discussing with the executive team how to manage their change better. The consultant was using the word "targets" to describe the people being asked to change. At the end of the day, after all the vice presidents left the room, the president of the bank confronted the consultant, pointing an angry finger in her face. "At this bank, we do not and will not use the offensive term 'targets.' We will call them 'change partners.'"

The boss had spoken, and loudly. Our consultant didn't argue: it was the president's bank and he could call the people whatever he chose. What the president and the consultant did not know was that their conversation had not been private. One of the vice presidents had heard the exchange through a crack in the boardroom door as he came back to retrieve his forgotten cellphone.

The next morning, the vice presidents and their boss returned to the boardroom for more discussions about the practice of change management. Given the conservative banking environment, all the men and women always wore dark suits, and crisp white shirts and ties, or blouses and scarves. But not today. Each of the vice presidents was wearing a suit, but they all had what looked like black T-shirts underneath. When the consultant explained that they would be using the term "change partners" instead of "targets" from now on, one brave soul looked the president straight in the eye and said, "With all due respect, sir, we don't feel much like change partners. We don't actually want to make this change, but we don't feel like we have a choice. At this point, we all think that the word 'target' is more appropriate." And with that, all the vice presidents stood up, took off their suit jackets, turned around and revealed big red bull's eyes, or targets, painted on the backs of the black T-shirts they were wearing.

Needless to say, the president got the message. It took three years before the majority of employees at the bank fully embraced the change, by which time the president was able to give them the new label "change partners." When he did so, the targets finally felt comfortable with this term.

The fundamental assumption underlying effective change management is that the people who are targets make a choice – they choose either to support the change or to resist it. Many managers initially disagree with this. "They don't have a choice. They have to change. If they don't, I'll fire them!" And therein lies the choice. The target of such a change can either choose to change or choose to be fired. However unfair this sounds, it is still a choice.

If you, as the change agent, are lucky, the resistant targets will admit that they oppose the change. Then you know what you are up against. But all too often, because it is too risky to admit that they are going to resist, targets keep their true feelings hidden. (This applies even when their resistance is legitimate – for example, when it results from a lack of information, or the fact that the desired state will result in downsizing and some people will lose their jobs.) "Does everyone agree that we need to make this change?" the vice president asks in the big meeting announcing the change. Every head nods in agreement. Then a quarter of the people who attended go out and, consciously or unconsciously, proceed to work against the change behind the vice president's back.

The targets can only make an informed choice about the change if you, as change agent, provide them with all the necessary information. However, if you find that people are choosing to resist, you cannot immediately take the blame. Nor must you automatically jump to the conclusion that the targets are being deliberately obstructive. Often, resistance is the first step in the normal, logical process that brings people to the point where they make their choice. Your task is to help them get past such resistance to a place where they can make up their minds thoughtfully and objectively. Your job is not to *make* everyone change. Rather, it is to set up an environment in which people can make their choice consciously, without excess emotion and with due consideration and attention.

If you imagine yourself in the shoes of the people being asked to change and consider how they will react, you can roughly predict the potential for resistance. Accept that the targets'

resistance makes sense from their perspective. Encourage the targets to tell you what their issues are and what they need in order to make a decision based on facts and reality, not on rumor and speculation.

Enabling the targets to graduate from being targets of the change to being partners in the change process is worth every effort because it dramatically increases the potential for your change to be successful. And once the targets have experienced one successful change, they will be more likely to support future changes.

As change agent you are responsible for coaching people in the change, and for this, as we have said, you need to be able to empathize with their perspectives and take time to help them through their problems. You need to listen and respond well – and sometimes read between the lines.

Seek out examples of two distinct categories of people. Look for those who welcome change, and are keen to play a helpful role within the change process. By recruiting such people as your allies, you can harness their energies. However, it's equally important to seek out those who are resistant to change. It's part of your job to ease the path for these conscripts and make them start to feel like volunteers.

Now let's look at some target reactions that you may encounter and consider strategies for dealing with them.

1. People feel anxious about the change and self-conscious because they don't know how to do things the new way. They fear being shown to lack skills.

Strategy: Acknowledge this as a legitimate reaction and assure the targets that they will be given any training that they need to enable them to perform well in the desired state. Take the targets step by step through their new roles, patiently explaining their job descriptions. Explain how any training will be given. Ask them if they feel that they may need further training, whether to brush up on neglected skills or to learn new ones. If you are offering in-house training sessions, speak to the trainers and ask them to be sympathetic to the targets' particular difficulties and needs.

2. People think first about what they might have to give up, not what they might gain.

Strategy: As change agents who have already bought into the change, we might tend to talk it up. However, don't try too hard initially to sell the benefits of the desired state: instead begin by acknowledging the value the old order provided in the past. Then convey the view that to stay healthy it's important to respond to changing conditions. And you could stress one new gain in particular, which easily outweighs whatever is lost: the knowledge that your organization will be in no danger of dying because it doesn't change. (For advice on targets whose jobs are in jeopardy, see p.51.)

3. People feel isolated, even if everyone else is going through the same change.

Strategy: Structure group activities around the change, to cement cooperation and a sense of shared purpose. For example, you could hold a group session to define more precisely some of the blurred edges of the desired state. Ask people to produce diagrams or charts showing possible ways in which new elements of the desired state will fit with each other and with old elements. Encourage people to discuss these different models and debate their pros and cons with a view to agreeing on a consensus.

4. People tune out because they have been bombarded with changes, and this is one change too many.

Strategy: Be clear in your management, concentrating on landmark stages rather than giving the impression that the change is a continuous state of upheaval. Go through the timeline for the change, emphasizing key dates and deadlines. Circulate summaries of the timeline so that everyone knows what has to happen when.

5. People absorb information at different rates, so they are at different levels of readiness for change.

Strategy: Recognize that some people are risk-takers, some take a balanced view, and others are cautious. With risk-takers, beware of their underestimating the difficulties of the challenge: talk them through all the stages of change, encouraging them to focus on anticipated situations. With the cautious ones, try to establish what specific concerns they have and address them patiently and constructively.

6. People say that they don't have enough resources, such as adequate funds or enough time.

Strategy: In any well-planned change, the provision of resources will be carefully budgeted, and spending against the budget will be monitored throughout the change process. Under the stress of change, people may overestimate the difficulties of their roles and feel that what they are being asked to do isn't possible within the time allotted. If you are uncertain how to proceed, the best approach is often to start this stage of change without extra resources, while being prepared to allocate them if it turns out to be necessary. If you do this, you will need to win support for the additional budget or perhaps for transferring funds from within the change budget.

7. People return to doing things the old way as soon as you take the pressure off them.

Strategy: Work to weave the new order inextricably into the organization's culture – for example, its approach to reward. Symbolic changes, such as redecorating the office, or upgrading furniture and equipment, can help. Prioritize actions that reflect the new order. Remember that as a manager, if you think in terms of the new current state, staff will find it impossible to communicate with you effectively unless they think in those terms too.

MULTIPLE ROLES AND HATS

As we have said, the sponsor will sometimes initiate the change, hand over its implementation to one or more change agents, and then receive regular progress reports on the change. Sometimes, however, the sponsor assumes a role that is managerial rather than presidential – in other words, they might take over the role of change agent, in part or in full.

At one extreme is the sponsor who briefs the change agent (whether as an individual or as a team leader) on the desired state and then leaves them to make a success of the transformation. At the other extreme is the sponsor who rolls up their sleeves right from the beginning and spends a great deal of time doing the job of the change agent.

When change agent and sponsor are working together to bring about the change, there are certain pitfalls that need to be avoided. One is a potential lack of clarity about who is responsible for what. It's usually a good idea for the main change agent to call a meeting with the sponsor to demarcate their responsibilities clearly. One way for the sponsor to operate is in offering help with tricky situations – for example, being the spokesperson for change in a difficult negotiation with staff. This could be combined with an agreement that the change agent may call upon the sponsor's hands-on services at any critical point within the delta state – for example, to deal with a reluctant target. Another way in which a sponsor might operate is to obtain the necessary resources from other sponsors.

All these permutations can work so long as clear ground rules are agreed beforehand. Sponsors should beware of "helpfully" taking actions that run counter to a change agent's strategy, especially in public, when the contradiction will be apparent to all. Sponsors who act as change agents can cause damage by confusing the targets or by duplicating their efforts unnecessarily. As a change agent working alongside a sponsor, you need to ensure that they have all the information needed for any managerial action. The sponsor has the responsibility to ensure that they know the difference between their own tasks and those of the change agent; and it is

one of the change agent's tasks to help the sponsor understand this difference. There is no substitute for regular and open communication between the two — it's particularly important to hold an initial meeting at which the job descriptions of the change agent and sponsor are clearly defined and distinguished from each other.

Another common example of multiple roles is the change agent who is also a target — because in fact this is true of almost all change agents. Despite any reservations about the change, you will need to work by example. You, like the targets, are affected by the change, and if you are seen to be dealing with major reorganization professionally, showing thoughtfulness and energy rather than panic and indecision, that can only be inspiring to those around you.

chapter 4

MAKING THE CHANGE WORK – COPING WITH PITFALLS

At the beginning of this book we set out three steps to well-managed change (see p.17): identifying potential resistance; overcoming that resistance with a three-point plan (learning, communication, reward); and formulating an action plan. We then went on to look at the basics of change, its operation as a process, and the roles and responsibilities of all involved.

In this chapter we continue to explore resistance. We address a critical variable – the impact that past change experiences might have had on staff. We discover how change can affect people physically, mentally and emotionally, and how to deal with these effects. We also learn how to assemble all the information we have gathered so far in a succinct, logical way so that we can make a realistic assessment of the resistance our change is likely to meet.

THE IMPACT OF THE PAST

No matter how severe the problems in the current state – nor how attractive the desired state may be – the way previous changes have been handled in your organization will influence the staff's decision as to whether to support or resist this change. They will have learned from past experience that change is managed either well or poorly in the organization. If they feel that they have been led into the fire of the delta state and left to burn there too many times, they will be extremely reluctant to endure such torments again. They may also have realized that change doesn't always get completed – perhaps, if they just duck their heads and play along for a while, management's ideas for change may well fade away again this time.

No change agent can ignore a history of badly managed change. We can try to sweep it under the rug or call the reintroduction of the same old change by a different name, but people will remember the upheaval they went through last time. For example, say you installed a new telephone system several years ago, with a direct line to each individual in order to speed up communications. However, only the heads of department had voicemail because this feature was an expensive extra. The result was that many workers suffered more disruption and lost more time answering

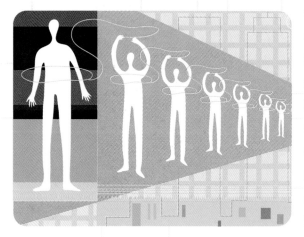

WORK SOLUTION 10

Evaluating Your Change History

Because the history of previous changes in your organization will influence the targets' decision to embrace or reject the current change, you need to determine how much of a problem that history will be. This exercise will help you to make an assessment.

1. Gather together a group of targets who have been involved in previous changes in the organization. Explain the kind of information you want and why you need it. Ask them to give you accounts of changes they have been through. Analyze your findings.

2. Use the checklist below and answer "yes" or "no" to each statement about how the organization responded.
   - Used consistently sound change-management strategies and tactics.
   - Rewarded those who handled the change well.
   - Always made sure communication, learning and reward strategies were in alignment.
   - Provided people with the resources they needed to make changes.
   - Faced up to failures and admitted mistakes.
   - Communicated the need for change throughout the organization.
   - Defined the desired state at each level of the organization.
   - Encouraged the expression of resistance and responded to it effectively.
   - Involved workers at all levels in the change process.
   - Recognized and celebrated small victories and ultimate successes.

3. Analyze your results. "No" answers will highlight areas where change has upset targets in the past. Focus on getting these right in this change.

colleagues' phones and taking messages when they were absent from their desks than with the old receptionist and switchboard system. Now, after suffering a year of falling productivity levels, management has decided to change again – to what is essentially a high-tech version of the old switchboard system.

And naturally enough, as with any organizational switch from one system to another, then back to something not unlike the first system, skeptical tongues start wagging. Sometimes, the rumor mill will even weave myths around the unsuccessful change – a whole set of humorous anecdotes whose details become more colorful with every retelling.

The key thing, for the sponsor or change agent, is not to feel too defensive about such murmurings. All management mistakes will generate negative reactions of some kind, and it

WE'RE DOING IT DIFFERENTLY THIS TIME

Any concerns among staff who have had bad experiences of previous changes within the same organization can be addressed by concentrating on these key features of the current plan:

- *We are following a carefully worked-out change-management process.*

- *We will be giving everyone the information, training and support they will need for a smooth, successful change.*

- *We invite everyone to bring to the change your own unique experience and skills – and to make any suggestions you may have for making the change easier, more cost-effective and more rewarding.*

- *We will keep you informed of progress in regular news bulletins.*

- *We will involve you in all stages of the change and welcome constructive feedback.*

is better to outweigh a negative with a positive than to try to undermine it with a rebuttal or counterattack. If mistakes have been made in the past, make it clear that all plans for the future are firm and confident. In the case of the example just mentioned, a strategic error has been made by senior management. There is little point in trying to deny that the first change was inaccurately conceived: indeed, denial will only make the situation worse by undermining management credibility. Better to acknowledge that the previous change was unsuccessful and to briefly itemize the reasons for its failure; and then move on to manage this change using the lessons learned from the previous changes and from this book.

Of course, an overriding factor in this example was insufficient foresight: the consequences of the change were not thought through in terms of how people actually worked. However, it's important that you choose your terms carefully when admitting to a blunder of this kind. To admit to an error of foresight can be perfectly acceptable – but unless convincing reasons are given, there is a danger that staff will infer only that their management is prone to making mistakes. Briefly explain the background to the "wrong turning" (a useful phrase). In the case of our example, perhaps it was assumed that voicemail for all would be unnecessary given that most staff worked mainly at their own desks. Go back beyond the mistake to one or two factors underlying it. Don't spend too long giving a convoluted explanation: concentrate more on your confidence that the current plan of action is absolutely right for the circumstances.

"The sudden prospect of change shakes me. I imagine my privileges disappearing. The basic premises of my working life are overturned: I now know that for some time I have been living with a false sense of security. I always believed our division was pulling its weight within the company structure, and now I see that its contribution has been below par. Sometimes I even feel guilty – have I been working hard enough, efficiently enough? Should I have noticed that things weren't ideal? Has my lack of awareness been noticed and frowned upon by my bosses? Change is likely, I guess, to create a new environment, new reporting lines, new responsibilities – and to throw me into contact with new people, or the same people in new roles. I've gotten used to the way things are – in a stable organizational setting I have learned to disguise my weaknesses and highlight my strengths. Maybe in the new order my weaknesses (the old ones, or even new ones I don't yet know about) will come to the fore and be noticed?" This is a hypothetical confessional extract from the journal of a change target, and is typical of those who react adversely to change.

As a change *agent*, you might be treating the change as a challenge and an adventure. It's good to experience a more fluid environment. You know that adaptability is essential to the success of your organization, and fluidity is a sign of adaptability. You have come to terms with your anxieties so that you can manage the change more effectively. However, some of the people you are managing through the change, like the writer of the journal quoted above, will still be

marooned in a state of resistance, and it is your job to help them through this into a more positive and constructive attitude.

When we are pushed into a change, our first reaction is to run away to avoid the change or to try to stop it – and this behavior, while a threat to the change, is logical and normal if you look at it through the eyes of those affected. They are not trying to destroy the organization. In fact the opposite is true: they are trying to protect it from you and your change.

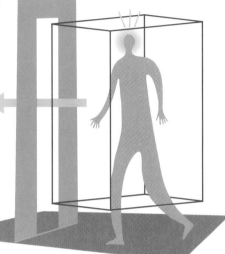

These initial reactions by staff are often difficult for sponsors and change agents to understand. If, for you, the change is not a threat and you are eager to leave the current state, you might find it hard to grasp why others don't see it the same way. That's the whole point of this discussion. Targets often *do* perceive change in a different way from sponsors and change agents, and react accordingly. Your job is not to dismiss those perceptions – they are legitimate interpretations by people affected by the change, based on how they see the world. You can't just brush aside these deeply-entrenched insecurities. Instead, you need to make an effort to recognize that if targets react initially with a strong need to flee from the change or to fight it, this is legitimate for them. Once targets feel that their concerns have been heard, they will be more likely to take the first step toward accepting the change.

RECOGNIZING RESISTANCE

In Chapter 1 you learned that overcoming resistance is vital if your change is to be successful (see p.17). Resistance comes in many forms. Sometimes it is deliberate. Or sometimes people impede the change unconsciously. From your previous experiences with change you may recognize some of the types of resistance we mention here.

Some staff will offer passive resistance, citing their workload, or some other factor, as a reason for being unable to participate. For example, they might say that they are too busy to go to the training sessions or to be part of the change team. They might try to avoid the change by going on vacation when you switch to the new system; or they might bring current work to a meeting about the change.

Other employees will be more actively resistant: they might ask the same questions over and over; they might challenge the data presented as part of the rationale for change; they might criticize the change agents. Some might even work to improve the current process after they know that it is going to be replaced.

This behavior varies according to which stage of change people are experiencing. In the current state they often act as if they haven't heard of or understood the change. In the delta state they will often ask whether they should prioritize their "urgent" work or learn the new process; and in the desired state they will often repeat that they don't understand the change and don't know how to work in the new way.

ANTICIPATING RESISTANCE

Even before a change is announced, it is possible for you as the change agent to anticipate reasons why people might resist. Use the following questionnaire to help you pinpoint those reasons.

Make photocopies of the list below. Now, taking a highlighter pen, highlight on one of the copies what you believe to be the three most likely reasons for resistance in each department that will undergo change. Then ask other members of the change team to do the same, and compare results. The more often the same reasons crop up, the higher the likelihood that you have accurately anticipated reasons for potential resistance.

Resistance to leaving the current state:
- *Don't see a need to change.*
- *Can't envision the desired state.*
- *Don't know how to change.*
- *Feel that the change is a criticism of performance.*
- *Would rather focus on a different change.*
- *Don't trust the change agents.*
- *Don't trust the sponsor.*
- *Are too comfortable in the current state.*
- *Have experienced failed or painful change in the past.*
- *Value current skills above new ones.*

Resistance to going through the delta state:
- *Have other priorities occupying their energy.*
- *Don't want a heavier workload.*
- *Don't think the organization can get through the transition.*
- *Think that the cost is too high.*
- *Think that the change is too disruptive.*
- *Think that the change requires too much effort.*
- *Feel that they are too little involved.*
- *Feel that the timing is bad.*
- *Feel that the reward is too low.*
- *Think that there are too many changes going on.*

Resistance to the desired state:
- *Would prefer a different solution.*
- *Fear unknown outcomes.*
- *Fear negative outcomes: loss of job/status/control/social structure.*
- *Worry about the change being irreversible.*
- *Feel that this change doesn't solve the problem.*
- *Feel that they won't be able to learn the new way.*
- *Can't see the relevance of the change to their work.*

THE CHANGE REACTION

We have seen that people required to change within an organization often value the current state and identify with that state emotionally, so that the prospect of change triggers a strong yet perfectly legitimate response in them – a reaction to what they perceive as a deep personal loss. Once such reactions have started to manifest themselves among the targets, how can a change agent take steps to minimize the turbulence and make people feel happier and better equipped to face the change ahead?

To put this question another way, how can the curve of a target's reactions to loss, as shown in the change resistance chart, opposite, be flattened?

Often the first response that a change agent has to deal with is immobilization – a kind of mental paralysis that some targets show when first confronting the prospect of change. The information just doesn't seem to sink in. Your job as change agent during this phase is to keep repeating the key facts of the change and the underlying reasons for it. "We need to cut overheads by 20 per cent to sustain an acceptable margin," the sponsor might have announced to everyone at a special staff meeting. "To do this we have to rationalize our spending on research and development, streamline our sales operation, and cut back our courier costs – which last year reached an unacceptable peak of around $10,000. We also have to explore new ways of getting sales materials to potential customers." The change agent's job is not only to put this plan into action to achieve the desired savings for the company, it is also to echo again and again to the targets the sponsor's essential message about cutting overheads, making it clear not just *how* people need to change but also *why*. Take every opportunity to reinforce the key points that lie behind the change until these points sink into the collective consciousness of the organization. Make every effort to support the change by anticipating possible arguments against it – for example, providing cost analyses that allow you to demonstrate to managers how their departments are clocking up unjustifiable spending.

The chart, below, shows how reaction may eventually progress from immobilization to denial. "Don't worry," says

THE RESISTANCE PROFILE OVER TIME

This graph shows how a target's resistance rises steeply from initial shock and immobilization up through denial to peak at anger. Then it falls again as the target moves quickly through negotiation and depression to exploration and, finally, to acceptance. The time it takes to reach acceptance depends both on the length and degree of the change and the level of the target's resistance.

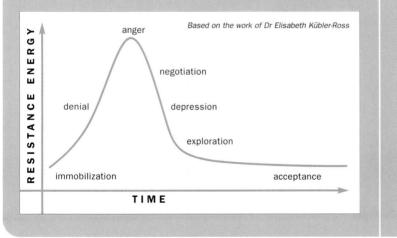

Based on the work of Dr Elisabeth Kübler-Ross

RESISTANCE ENERGY

anger

negotiation

denial

depression

exploration

immobilization

acceptance

TIME

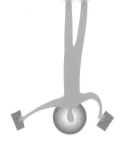

the target in the next phase of change psychology, "they won't do it. They don't have the nerve. They're just trying to scare us." But by this time you are showing that you mean what you say. For practicality's sake you have moved very quickly to break down the change into a series of discrete steps, which you are asking everyone to follow, according to a declared plan and timeline. Week by week the action steps are put into effect, without delay. The staff understand what is happening and when, and some of them are beginning to cooperate with the change.

However, in a certain proportion of the targets the denial phase has probably shaded into anger, and there may even be the occasional confrontation. You must make every attempt to defuse anger by allowing targets to express their true feelings. One way to do this is by holding private one-to-one meetings, which enable an employee to speak openly. When anger breaks out in such situations, you can allow it to run its course. In response, your best approach to such people is to state sympathetically that you understand their anger, because anger is a natural reaction to leaving the comfort of the current state. You might choose, if you wish, to go further than this, and show reluctant targets the change resistance graph on p.105 of this book. If you sense emotions below the surface, you might decide to draw them into the open by saying something like the following: "I know this change must be difficult for you. You have done a great job at making this department run smoothly for the last twelve years. All the hard work you have put into making improvements to the

WORK SOLUTION 11

Creating an Atmosphere of Trust

As change agent you need information about how targets are reacting to the change. The best way to get this information is to ask them in an atmosphere of trust in one-to-one or small group meetings.

1. Prepare the room for your meeting. If there's a desk in it, consider sitting on the same side as the target(s) to remove any physical barriers between you.

2. Start the meeting at the precise time you have agreed. (You need to show yourself as reliable and trustworthy.) Open the discussions by letting the target(s) know why you have called this meeting. Explain that you want to know what their concerns about the change are so that you can find ways in which to help them come to terms with the change. If appropriate, promise anonymity. Stress how it will benefit them to give you a better insight into their concerns and assure them that there will be no negative repercussions to them for sharing their thoughts and fears with you.

3. Make a conscious effort to keep your body language open and honest (no folded arms, or hand or leg jitters). Maintain eye contact throughout and listen attentively. Repeat back any statements to check that you have understood correctly and to let them know that you have heard what they are saying.

4. Conclude by inviting questions. Let the target(s) ask you anything about the change. Give complete and honest answers. Say that if anything comes to mind later, you have an open-door policy – they can approach you at any time.

production processes we are using today have generated great success. Is leaving the way we have always done things here going to be hard for you?"

Whenever anyone shows anger, or any other strong response, recognize the emotion as a legitimate expression of feeling – but be careful not to react emotionally yourself. It is useful to translate another person's emotion into the opinion that lies behind it; and then to engage with the opinion, not with the emotion. You might yourself feel a strong emotion – such as frustration – when dealing with a target who is being angry, or pessimistic, or in any other way negative about the change you have come to value. If so, try to "let go" of that emotion: let it pass through your thoughts, and remind yourself that as change agent you are paid to remain patient and supportive (though also firm and persuasive) in your dealings with others.

During the negotiating phase of the change reaction your job is to deal with any targets who do not accept the roles prescribed for them in the desired state. At this point in the change process it is important that the change agent is absolutely clear about which parts of the desired state are negotiable, as already determined (see p.45, Work Solution 5). Any target who tries to negotiate with you outside this predetermined area will need to be reminded that this aspect of the change is beyond negotiation.

Depression may set in when targets realize that the organization will *listen* to all their demands but will not agree to *concede* them all. With a heavy heart these targets face the certain prospect of the new order and the irretrievable loss of the old. Now, when people are depressed, they benefit from talking about it – so again you must allow them their say. Encourage them to talk things through with colleagues. In particular, encourage contact with those who are at the exploration and acceptance stages of the change cycle. Emphasize or bring forward the plus points of the change – for example, by initiating training programs well in advance of the actual requirements.

As targets explore the realities of the change, acknowledge the value of their cooperation. Build their confidence by praising every step they take toward "living" in the desired state. Thank them for all their efforts. As confidence grows there will be a moment of acceptance when they decide to give the change a chance.

CREATING AN INFOMATRIX

By now you have probably amassed a huge amount of information about the change, encompassing who might resist, why and how. We think you'll agree that it would be helpful to have it all in one place. We suggest that you take all the information you have gathered about potential resistance to the change from each target (or group of targets) and put it on a master chart. We call this master chart the InfoMatrix (see example, opposite).

Once you have entered all the information for each target or target group, you will be able to see, at a glance, where the potential pockets of resistance lie. This, in turn, will enable you to take action to reduce (or maybe even to prevent) that resistance by applying the strategies we discussed earlier (see pp.24–7).

The InfoMatrix will also help you to identify those employees who are likely to respond well to the change. These are your potential allies in making the change as smooth and painless as possible, and you might choose to consult with them early on to obtain valuable perspectives on the process.

It's a good idea to draw up an InfoMatrix in the planning stages, to enable you to make judgments about the nature of the challenge that lies ahead. You can then update the chart as the change plan is put into practice.

If you use the numerical scoring system suggested on the opposite page (in the italic type), it will enable you to see immediately both the strengths and weaknesses within your change plan in terms of resistance or acceptance.

HOW TO DRAW UP AN INFOMATRIX

The InfoMatrix is your summary, for each target group, of how they are likely to respond to the change. You can use this overview to assess the timing and difficulty of the change process.

Make your chart either on paper or within a computer spreadsheet. Assign a score on a scale of 1 to 10 for each question – 1 being a resounding no and 10 a resounding yes. The lowest numbers represent the issues you will need to address through communication, learning and rewards.

NAME OF TARGET GROUP:

STAGES OF CHANGE	**Current**	Do they see a need to make a change of some kind?	Do the problems of the current state cause them discomfort?	Will the benefits of the change outweigh the drawbacks?
	Desired	Will they see this change as a good solution?	Will they be able to work effectively in the desired state?	Will they find job satisfaction in the desired state?
	Delta	Will they tolerate disturbance and compromise?	Will they cope with the workload of the change?	Will productivity remain high during the change?
KEY ROLES	**Sponsors**	Do they have faith in the managers?	Do they believe the change is in the right hands?	Will they be offered the necessary support and resources?
	Change Agents	Do they accept the change?	Do they have the necessary skills and experience?	Are they respected by staff?
	Targets	Will they show a reaction to the change?	Are they comfortable with change in general?	Will they be supportive and cooperative in the change?
CRITICAL VARIABLES	**Culture**	Are the core beliefs of the organization appropriate?	Is the culture supportive of the individual?	Is communication within the organization good?
	History	Have people responded well to previous changes?	Do people understand how the organization has evolved?	Has the management been effective in implementing previous changes?

chapter 5

THE SAFETY NETS

People going through a change often feel as though they are walking along a tightrope strung across a deep chasm that divides the current state and the desired state. Your job as a change agent is to provide the safety nets that make it possible for staff to get across that chasm without fear and with the confidence that comes from knowing that if they experience any problems, they can count on your help and support.

So far you have been working on step 1 of a well-managed change: gauging potential reactions to the change. This chapter guides you through step 2 of the change project: designing ways to minimize resistance and maximize support.

There are three safety nets that you can put in place to make it easier for targets to choose to change, and to change successfully. Those safety nets are the communication, learning and reward plans.

THE FIRST SAFETY NET:
THE COMMUNICATION PLAN

During a change, those affected have an almost unquenchable thirst for knowledge. People want to know why the change is happening, what things are going to look like when the change is finished, and how the organization is going about the process of changing. It is your job to provide that information via the communication plan (see Work Solution, opposite), which identifies what is to be communicated, to whom, how, when and at what cost, throughout the change.

It is important that the information you communicate is straightforward and honest. Take this opportunity to address any false rumors circulating, such as an unfounded suspicion that the organization is about to be bought out. However,

if, for example, rumors about future job cuts are true, then say so, using language that is direct, balanced and objective. Trying to cover up such facts will only result in your losing credibility in the long term. Similarly, if the reason for change is unpleasant, the staff still need to hear it. You might have to explain to them that a competitor has broken through the price barrier and is selling a product for much less than your version, and that therefore you need to reduce costs in order to bring your prices down. It also helps

WORK SOLUTION 12

Drawing up the Communication Plan

On paper or on a spreadsheet, create three tables for each target group, each with the following four labels across the top: Information Required; Communication Type; Timing; Cost. One table covers the initial phase of the change; one the delta or implementation phase; and one the final phase, in which the desired state becomes the new current state.

1. In each table, under "Information Required" list the information the targets are going to need in that phase of the change. Bear in mind, when deciding on the content of your communication plan, that some of the staff with whom you need to communicate may have only a hazy picture of aspects of the organization that lie outside their own narrow field of concern.

2. Under the heading "Communication Type" describe how the information will be shared (at a meeting or via a memo, a newsletter, and so on). For example, you might choose to hold a departmental meeting, as well as display informative posters around the department concerned.

3. Under "Timing" state when communication should occur. Fix a date for the departmental meeting, and also arrange a date by which the posters should be ordered so they can be put up a few days in advance of the meeting.

4. Under "Cost" note the cost of that communication. For example, in the above situation you would estimate the cost of the design and printing of the posters.

to place the organization's predicament in the context of the broader commercial picture. Try to help targets to understand the situation and how it is being handled.

When you have laid out the communication plan, review how and by whom the messages will be conveyed. When a change is being explained to staff, this is always a good opportunity to present an up-to-date thumbnail portrait of the organization's activities and its place in the scheme of things. People will welcome such a summary: ideally it will remind them of what they might have forgotten about the current state, or tell them what they never knew, as well as anticipating their questions about the desired state. Such overviews are ideally presented in the form of a speech by the sponsor.

Of course, the ways in which various change agents express the communication plan's messages may be different. For example, an executive-level manager might speak about the change as it relates to the business goals of the organization, while the supervisor of accounts might talk about the fact that the change will require their team to learn a new computer application. One message is strategic, the other is tactical, but each must include the same core information. The Work Solution opposite will show you how to achieve such consistency.

WORK SOLUTION 13

Speaking with One Voice

If the communication plan is to achieve its aim of securing the support of all the people who will be affected by the change, consistency is crucial. In practice, this means that all messages delivered through speeches, meetings, memos, articles in the newsletter and casual hallway conversations should relay the same basic information. How can you help the sponsor and change agents – including yourself – to deliver a consistent message?

1. Design a core message to be used by everyone who communicates as a sponsor of the change or as a change agent. The message must clearly answer the three core questions: Why do we have to change? What will our organization or department look like when the change is completed? How will we get from where we are today to this desired state? Keep the answers as brief and clear as possible – try to limit each statement to one or two sentences.

2. Take the time to learn this core message by heart. You need to be able to relay it confidently (and adapt it quickly and easily, if necessary, to suit any audience) without having to refer to notes. You will often want to recapitulate the main points all through the change process.

3. Present the core message to the sponsor and other change agents who will be delivering it and explain why you have written it. Tell them why it is important that they don't deviate from those three points when communicating about the change. Be prepared to adapt and modify the message as a result of their feedback; they also need to feel comfortable with the message if they are to deliver it effectively.

A key to the success of the communication plan is getting people to trust its messages. They may have learned from past changes not to believe information they are given or to suspect that the information is incomplete.

To get past that mistrust the plan must include ways by which employees can test the validity or accuracy of its messages. It's important to allow questions: any speech given without an opportunity for listeners to air their concerns will be seen as a showpiece, which will only alienate staff. Moreover, all questions need to be taken seriously – even when they're based on fundamental errors of information and logic. As a change agent, you must listen patiently and try to tease out the genuine points. However, a CEO who asks 457 people in a large meeting whether anyone has a question about the change may be met with silence, probably because nobody wants to appear not to have understood the boss, or seem to be resistant in front of them. Holding small, informal meetings and/or asking for anonymous written feedback may produce more questions and comments. Remember always to react to the feedback you receive. Ensuring that everyone feels like partners in a two-way communication process will go a long way toward gaining commitment to the change.

WORK SOLUTION 14

Giving Staff a Voice

It is important that you verify the targets' understanding of each message sent about the change and give them an opportunity to seek clarification and share their reactions to the information. Here are some suggestions to help you do this.

1. Hold a "town-hall" meeting – this is a small group meeting, to which the sponsor and key targets are invited. The targets have the option of submitting written questions or comments for discussion to the sponsor before the meeting (if questions have to be posed during the meeting, the targets may feel intimidated and withhold negative feedback).

2. Organize a "brown-bag" lunch – a senior manager and the targets all bring their lunch and chat as they eat together in a room that has been specially set aside. This encourages everyone to talk as equals and helps create an atmosphere in which people feel relaxed enough to give honest feedback about the change.

3. After each landmark communication, be that via memo, meeting or article printed in the organization's newsletter, consider sending each employee an electronic survey about the communication, to be completed and submitted anonymously. While this can be a time-consuming operation, the payback can be considerable. Such a survey allows you not only to find out if you, or whoever delivered the message, were successful in conveying it, but also to discover exactly what people felt about its content and the way in which it was delivered.

THE SECOND SAFETY NET:
THE LEARNING PLAN

It's not enough to know why a change is needed, what it will entail and how it should be implemented. Frequently the desired state requires people to be able to do new things they have never done before. That means they need training.

The learning plan identifies the skills and/or knowledge required by each target group throughout the change. It determines when they need that training, how it will be delivered and assessed, by whom and at what cost.

The learning plan should cover both in-house systems individual to your organization and generic skills applicable in your industry. The latter can be taught by external trainers, whereas the former will need to be conveyed in in-house seminars or one-to-one sessions.

Consider sending extra people – for example, back-up staff to cover for principal staff who are off sick or on vacation – on the same training course at the same time. With in-house training, multiple attendance will be less costly than it is when staff are sent for outside training, and even where good external courses are available it may be better financially and logistically to organize customized in-house training.

To avoid resentment among targets, make sure that you and the

WORK SOLUTION 15

Drawing Up the Learning Plan

The learning plan sets out in detail the kind of training each target or target group will need. On paper or on a spreadsheet, create a table for each target or target group with the following seven headings across the top: Name of Target/Target Group; Knowledge/Skill Required; Needed By; When; How; Assessment; and Cost. Fill in the data for each target or target group by working through the steps outlined below.

1. Write the name of the individual or group under "Target/Target Group." Under "Knowledge/Skill Required" describe the new knowledge or skills that these targets are going to need in the delta and/or desired states. For example, your organization's accounts clerks may need to learn how to archive data from the current computer system and how to use the new system.

2. Under "Needed By" note when the targets will start using the new skills.

3. Under "When" plot the timing of the training course – when will it start and finish? How many hours' training should it involve?

4. Under "How" explain the kind of training required – will it be on an individual basis or in group classes with a trainer? Will it be in- or out-of-house?

5. Under "Assessment" describe how the gap between the targets' current and required levels of capability will be assessed after the training. For example, will the clerks assess their own progress? Or will they be formally tested?

6. Under "Cost" note how much the training will cost your organization. (If you are using external training, ask them to supply an estimate.)

other change agents and sponsors also go on training courses, if appropriate, and are seen to develop new skills.

Remember that the timing of training programs is crucial. If, say, training occurs too long before the new computers are installed, employees could have lost the motivation provided by the course, or, worse still, forgotten everything they learned by the time their new skills are required.

Learning to Get through the Delta

As a change agent, you need to ensure that people become flexible, adaptable and tolerant enough to deal with the state of flux that is the delta phase of change. In order to do this, you must start with yourself – after all, you are also a target of the change.

The delta state involves ambiguity and volatility, and at times may even approach the chaotic. A positive attitude will help you cope with this. Try to recall regularly why the old way is no longer appropriate, and focus on the advantages the desired state will offer. Instead of worrying about the change, revel in the challenge. Remind yourself daily that some confusion in the delta state is normal and will result in a finely-tuned desired state later.

Look, too, for opportunities to hone new working methods as they are being put in place, so that the desired state will be as near ideal as possible. Enjoy being part of the team that is pulling together to make the change a reality. And make the most of this chance to learn new skills.

You also need to build resilience and tolerance for the delta state in your targets. Make sure that your learning plan includes opportunities for people to acquire these qualities. Share any reservations that you yourself had initially. Explain how you overcame these reservations and how they, like you, can learn to see the positive aspects of the delta state.

LEARNING NECESSITIES

Everyone involved in the change – sponsor(s), change agent(s) and targets – must be given the chance to find out about the change.

They also need to learn how to manage the delta state, both emotionally (how to cope with the state of flux) and practically (how to juggle the old and new work simultaneously). Everyone should be able to obtain the knowledge and skills necessary to survive in the desired state – for example, how to use the new computer software. As the diagram below shows, the learning plan (see pp.120–21) should provide an overview of all the education that the targets require to deal successfully with each of the three stages of the change.

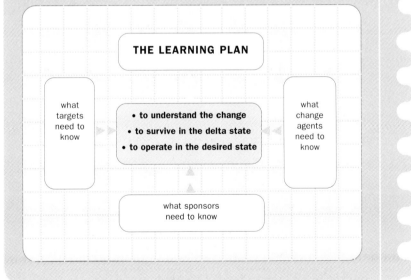

THE LEARNING PLAN

what targets need to know

- **to understand the change**
- **to survive in the delta state**
- **to operate in the desired state**

what change agents need to know

what sponsors need to know

THE THIRD SAFETY NET: THE REWARD PLAN

You now have a communication plan that enables you to inform people effectively about the change and a learning plan so that you can provide staff with the skill and knowledge to perform successfully in the desired state. However, before employees can decide whether or not they will support the change, there are two more critical questions to which they will need to have clear answers: Will you encourage me through the delta if I decide to change? And what's in it for me, personally?

The reward plan addresses both these issues. The first part of the plan, which we will discuss here, allows you to identify which behavior should be recognized and rewarded in the delta state and by what means. The second part of the plan consists of a new performance-management strategy, which will be applied in the desired state (for more on this topic, see pp.128–9).

People moving toward the desired state achieve much more if the change agents and the sponsors recognize the efforts that they make in the most difficult stage of the change – the delta state. As a change agent you need to decide on the answers to two key questions. First, what should be the criteria for rewarding individual and group effort in the delta state? And second, what should those rewards consist of?

The delta state is characterized by a series of distinct steps according to the schedule being followed. Some of these steps will have symbolic importance as the end of the old way of doing things and the beginning of the new way of doing things. Whenever a target group reaches one of these milestones, that is the time for appropriate rewards to be triggered. Rewarding people on such occasions sends out a clear message that the management appreciates their efforts under the extraordinary circumstances of the delta. It's also apt to celebrate the major achievements of the change, and especially its successful conclusion, by a social event such as a party, a grand picnic, or the like.

Where a change has caused massive disruption for a period – for example, a temporary office move while the headquarters is being refurbished – it is important to honor that extraordinary effort. One way to do this might be to organize a celebration to mark the re-opening of the office. Or alternatively you could show your appreciation by giving a few extra days off to all those who have worked long days packing and unpacking.

Change agents and sponsors should always be aware of the importance attached by staff to even small, symbolic gestures of thanks. If managers think that the change has been costly, and the business simply can't afford to give a bonus or

thankyou present to everyone, they should reconsider, because staff loyalty is the most positive feature of an organization's culture. Better to give something small, with a sincere personal message, than nothing at all. All employees appreciate it when management gives, say, some flowers and a card to someone at a junior level who has put in the extra effort needed to make the logistics of the change work smoothly.

Most targets, if asked how they would like to be rewarded for their contribution to achieving the desired state, would choose a salary raise or a bonus. Certainly, where change happens in response to opportunities rather than threats, the sponsors or change agents might feel that monetary recognition is appropriate – perhaps to reflect extra responsibilities taken on by certain individuals. Even where jobs have been lost, it makes sound commercial sense to give due financial reward in cases where, for example, two jobs are now being covered by one individual.

WORK SOLUTION 16

Designing Rewards for the Delta State

There are countless ways in which you can recognize people's efforts and hard work in the delta state. Rewards need not necessarily be expensive or elaborate – in fact, creative, fun ways of saying thankyou that also serve to reinforce team spirit often work best. Below are some ideas that you might like to consider. Remember that even though you, as the change agent, will be the one to plan which gestures should be made and when, it should be the change sponsors who actually present the rewards.

1. Organize a token system. For example, when targets complete each module of a multi-course training curriculum, give each of them a token (a coin or chip). Targets can collect all the chips and, when they have completed the curriculum, exchange them for a small gift, such as a complimentary dinner-for-two voucher.

2. If progress through the delta has become bogged down, try holding a "Save the Change" campaign in the cafeteria. Arrange for free high-energy foods and vitamins for all to symbolize the energy that targets are expending on implementing the change. Follow up with free desserts as a thank you for all the effort everyone has made to date. Ask a sponsor to make a short speech congratulating everyone on the progress made so far and encouraging them to keep up their efforts until the organization has reached the desired state.

3. Time off is always a welcome reward – you could send everyone home early on a specified day to celebrate the fact that the new procedures are in place and being used by, say, 95 per cent of the workers. Let the targets know what you are planning in advance so that they can make personal plans for that time.

LOOKING TO THE FUTURE: REWARDS IN THE DESIRED STATE

The second part of the reward plan sets out how managers will recognize and reward job performance in the desired state. This part of the plan should be based on your organization's existing performance-management system. That may be a formal system, with regularly scheduled reviews and a process for determining yearly goals and assessing achievement. Or it may be an informal system that consists of staff watching to see what makes the boss smile or frown. Whichever system operates in your organization, people do their job with the expectation that, if they do it "right," they will be rewarded. In the new, desired state, some of the "right" ways to work are going to disappear; some will be replaced. Therefore, the measures of success must change accordingly.

To design this part of the reward plan, you need to consider what is currently being rewarded and what should be rewarded in the desired state. Make a list of the people whose jobs will change. Determine exactly how their jobs will change and what the new performance measures will be. (If your organization has a human resources department, you will need to ask them to help with the job description and the performance-management process.) Even in organizations that operate a formal performance-management system, there is often a set of unofficial criteria for assessing the quality and quantity of performance. For example, the performance measure may be "Follow written inventory ordering procedures." But the unwritten rule may be, "If you think you might need 20, order 30 just in case." In the desired state

the procedure for determining what the target needs to order will be stricter. But if the old behavior still gets approval from the boss, the target may well choose not to change. It is therefore important that the sponsors sanction the new performance measures and agree to reinforce them. Before reaching the desired state, you will probably need to meet with the sponsors to gain approval for the new reward criteria.

No one can expect the desired state to be a paradise, where all are given the rewards they think they deserve and no one is discontented after each performance review. Yet given that your organization is spending time, money and energy on reaching the desired state, there is no point in undoing all that good work by demotivating people as a result of failing to recognize their performance.

COMPLETING THE PLANS

You are now in a position to review the data contained in the communication, learning and reward plans you have drawn up. With the three plans laid out in front of you, work out how much all the communication, training and rewards will cost the organization in total. Can this cost be justified? What will the organization get in return? Will the change happen faster? With less resistance?

Now ask yourself whether there is anything you have forgotten that would make it easier for people to deal with this change? Is there anything you could do to reduce the effort and the cost involved? For example, could you cut down on the software licenses you need to buy, or fine-tune the training program to render it more efficient and streamlined? Once you are satisfied that your plans are complete, you can go on to build a detailed action, or implementation, plan, which we will discuss in Chapter 6.

WORK SOLUTION 17

Closing the Planning Cycle

It is now time to take action – to implement the plan. Before you do, take one last look at what you have accomplished in order to pinpoint insights that could be useful in managing future changes.

1. Review what you have done up to this point: the discussions you have had with colleagues and the three change plans you have produced. Reflect on what you have learned as a change target. Taking a pen and paper, draw up a list of insights you have gained into your own reactions to change. Next to each item note what you will do with that insight as you progress through this and future changes. Review your initial reservations about the change. Did you initially think that some aspects of the current state should be protected from change? Did you disagree with the timing of the change? What are your thoughts now?

2. Draw up a list of any insights you have gained so far from your role as a change agent. Next to each item on the list note what you will do with that insight as you progress through this and future changes. For example, you might note down that your early messages about the change were too brief, which led to misunderstandings. In future you might resolve to include all the information targets need and always check that they have understood the message.

3. Think about what you have discovered about your organization's ability to make change happen. Is the way this change is being handled going to improve that ability? Note down any ways you can think of in which you could help the organization to record the lessons you have learned and render them useful for the next change.

chapter 6

THE MASTER ACTION PLAN

When you reach this point in your change project most of your work – that is, actually planning the change – is now done. You know who the targets are and what their resistance issues might be and you have designed the actions that will reduce or eliminate that resistance. Now it is time to make the change actually happen. As you move through the implementation phase of the change and work your way through the delta state, you will be putting into practice the communication, learning and reward plans that you set up in Chapter 5.

This chapter explores the master action plan – the third and final step in the process we defined on p.17 and the key to making the next phase of the change a success. The plan consists of three elements: a timeline, a reporting format and a process for changing the change.

THE TIMELINE

Time is one of the most important assets of any business and particularly of a business in change. The smooth running of a change project depends on a chain of events happening in the right order and at the right time. For example, the new office furniture must be delivered before the new computers appear; the information about what is changing needs to be circulated before everyone goes off to a training class. Unless the timing of these events is carefully planned in advance, the change itself will be undermined, and may even collapse.

In the chart below we set out a simplified version of a timeline – a vital tool that enables you to ensure that what has to be done gets done, in the right order, and is finished by the deadline set by the organization for achieving the desired state.

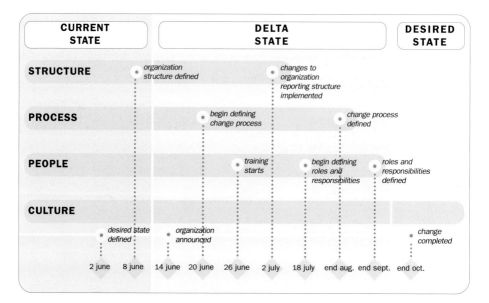

WORK SOLUTION 18

Reviewing the Change Calendar and the Timeline

It's time to review the change calendar you produced earlier (see p.55). You should check that both the date for reaching the desired state and the deadlines for the action steps you need to take between the current and desired state are still viable and correspond with the deadlines you have charted on your timeline. You then need to review the timeline with others involved in the change.

1. Write the actions you have identified since Chapter 2 in the left-hand column of the change calendar. Then enter them on the timeline. Check that the planned sequence of actions will allow them all to be completed by the date on which you should reach the desired state.

2. Examine the timeline to determine whether the sequence loads too much work into any particular time interval. If you know of other change projects or heavy assignments that will be impacting upon people, ask to see the relevant timelines and look for clashes where a particular group of workers will be involved in too many change activities at once.

3. Review the timeline with all the key change agents to test your assumptions about the sequence and logic of the time you have allocated.

4. Review the timeline with the Steering Team, if there is one (see pp.32–3) to ensure that they will support it and be willing to oversee the individual actions.

5. Display the change calendar and the timeline where everyone working on the change can see them.

To produce your timeline, create a horizontal base line, starting at the current state, and ending with the date by which the change should be complete. Label the intervening months/quarters/weeks/days (whatever makes sense for your project) with the major milestones that you have to reach by certain dates. In addition to all the actions that are identified in the communication, learning and reward plans (omitted in our simplified example), these deadlines might include the dates by which desks for the new location should be ordered and then delivered, when the new procedure manuals should be printed and distributed, and so on.

Pin up your timeline where everyone in the change team can see it. Check progress along the timeline at least once a week. If deadlines are missed, ask yourself whether the whole calendar will have to be rescheduled or whether this is merely a localized problem that does not affect the timing of other activities. Make sure everyone knows the consequences of missed deadlines, such as extra costs and the loss of customers to whom you can't deliver as agreed. However, by the same token you should ensure that everyone is aware of the favorable results of completing the change project early – such as money saved, customer satisfaction, and so on. Motivate everyone to engage fully with the timeline by displaying it in a place where people can discuss it and, hopefully, celebrate their achievement of its dictates.

As the implementation phase of the change approaches, examine your time-management skills and ask yourself whether you could improve them. (You will certainly need

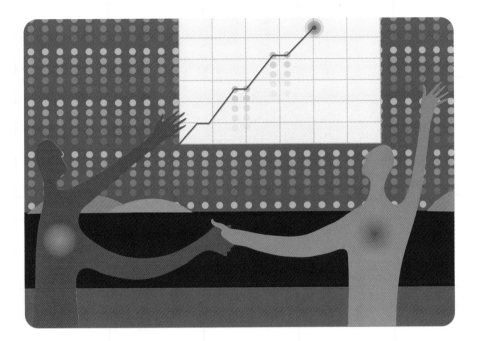

to put them to full use if you are managing a change project as well as doing your normal job.) For example, you may realize that the meetings you chair often start late or run over time. Before the next meeting make sure everyone knows that you expect them to arrive punctually. Begin at the designated time, even if only two people are present (the others will have to catch up when they get there), and stick to the agenda – don't let people wander off the point or ramble. Similarly, if you have noticed that targets regularly submit reports, send out mailshots to customers or install new software later than you requested, explain the importance of timing to the change project and warn them how such delays impact upon everyone else.

DESIGNING A REPORT FORMAT

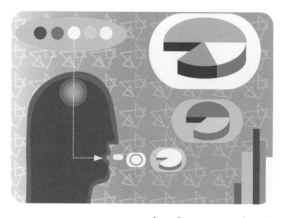

You, your team members if you are working with other change agents, and your management need to review the progress of the change on a regular basis. You may decide on the basis of this review to re-brief the targets, to mobilize additional resources – or even make changes to the desired state. A status report, regularly updated, provides a useful snapshot of how the project is going. As a change agent, you may choose to set up a formalized monitoring process to ensure that every aspect of the change is running according to plan – or that the plan is being modified where necessary. The status report should cover all the important aspects of the change. Is the project on schedule? Is it on budget? Are people fulfilling their responsibilities? Do changes need to be made to the change process? Is the resistance greater or less than anticipated? Are the action plans to mitigate resistance working? Does the desired state need refining?

We recommend building the report within a spreadsheet that lists the elements of the change process down the left column, as illustrated opposite. In the box to the right of each of these categories note the status of each and highlight any areas of concern. You can use three different colors to represent the three categories of high, medium and low risk as a means of communicating the relative status of each element.

STATUS REPORT FOR FUND-RAISING DEPARTMENT CHANGE PROJECT

CURRENT STATE	*Definition of the current state and reason for change approved by Steering Team. Action: give first indication of change to targets.*
DELTA STATE	*Four sub-projects identified as path to desired state. Action: determine timeline for each sub-project.*
DESIRED STATE	*Definition of desired state approved by the Steering Team. Action: plan formal statement for targets.*
SPONSOR	*Requires weekly updates. Action: suggest format for updates.*
CHANGE AGENTS	*Change Management Team leader's role not yet defined. Action: hold Change Management Team meeting to discuss this, then ask for meeting with sponsor.*
TARGETS	*Rumors spreading. Action: notify targets formally about change.*
CULTURE	*Some employees believe current fund-raising techniques are the only way to raise funds.*
HISTORY	*Report done on last big change. Action: change agents to discuss.*
RESISTANCE	*Some resistance anticipated in 50 per cent of staff.*
COMMUNICATION SYSTEM	*Plan needed. Action: quash rumors by issuing formal statement, then prepare detailed plan.*
LEARNING SYSTEM	*Plan needed. Action: must include retraining in negotiation techniques.*
REWARD SYSTEM	*Plan needed. Action: discuss voucher system and celebration of change milestones.*

    ○ Low Risk   ◔ Med Risk   ● High Risk

CHANGING THE CHANGE

Various possible factors may impinge on your change as you proceed to plan it and then implement it. For one thing, the business case underlying the change may itself be changing. A dramatic example of this would be the sudden and unexpected success of a new product line – say, a range of traditional kitchenware – taking a company out of breaking even into healthy profit for the year. The revenue from the new product would have been forecast at the time of planning the change, but let us say that there was a high level of uncertainty associated with it.

A farsighted company might have delayed committing to the change plan until some indications were obtained of how fat the order book for the new product was likely to be. Or the CEO might have decided to progress down the change route anyway, knowing that if the product were only moderately successful it would be necessary to make the change without delay. Or then again the success of the product might be beyond the company's wildest dreams – as it might be if this kitchenware were recommended on primetime TV by a famous chef. Then there is the fourth possibility, that the kitchenware line is run from a particularly efficient department and rationalizing the rest of the company still makes sound business sense. Alongside this rationalization a further change might now be required – to expand the capacity of the kitchenware department to satisfy the unprecedented demand for the new range. Some of the staff who were due for redundancy under the first version of the change plan might be retrained and redeployed in the kitchenware

department. So the change is subjected to change, in a conscious and careful manner.

Other factors that might require the modification of a change plan include dramatic currency fluctuations, changes in the law (affecting, say, taxation policy or health and safety regulations) and important individuals changing jobs.

Living with such ambiguities is a key part of your job. If it's possible to predict that certain eventualities have more than a slight chance of materializing, try to make contingency arrangements within your change plan. Mark the assessment dates on your timeline. Track changes in your regular status reports. If necessary, adjust the schedule for change to allow for the new factors. All organizations exist in a world of flux, and you must learn to have no qualms about changing the change when necessary.

chapter 7

THE CYCLE OF CHANGE

In every organization you will hear stories of a successfully implemented change project that later collapsed. For months the change agents worked on the design of the desired state. They then spent even longer implementing that design. Finally it was time to celebrate success with a victory party, for they had reached the desired state. However, when they checked back on the people working in that new state six months later, they found that the organization looked exactly as it had prior to the change. As soon as those annoying change agents had left, the people who had been the targets of the change had modified the new processes, and returned to old habits until they had got things almost entirely back to "normal."

In this chapter we learn how to ensure that the desired state, which everyone has worked so hard to install, is sustained in the long term.

MONITORING THE "NEW" CURRENT STATE

Before you can leave the scene of the change, you need to examine your organization's structure to determine who would be the best person to watch over the "new" current state and deal with any changes in it.

The change monitor, of course, might be you, the change agent. Naturally, whoever is doing the monitoring must have a good view of the operation impacted by the new current state, and this usually means having managerial responsibility over that particular area. This person may delegate the job of collecting information to someone who reports to them. However, it remains their responsibility to find out how the new current state is performing and to pass the message up along the chain of command. One possibility is that all department heads, having gathered data in this way, report to their divisional head, a senior manager, on a monthly basis. The process of regular monitoring continues until everyone is satisfied that the new current state is completely stable.

In Work Solution 5 (p.45) you identified the desired state by addressing two key questions. First, you considered which elements of the desired state were final and therefore not subject to further change without launching a new change project. Second, you asked what aspects could be open to adjustment, or even to removal – in other words, what was subject to further change?

Your answers to the above questions provide you with the foundation for monitoring the desired state, or what will now be known as the new current state. The change monitor will check whether those elements that were determined

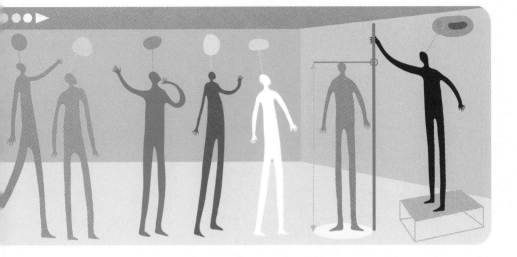

as fixed are staying that way. This might involve regularly testing the quality of the products coming off the production line, or conducting a periodic customer survey to make sure that there is an acceptable level of customer satisfaction.

The areas already identified as being subject to continuous improvement – such as processes – require careful monitoring by someone who can spot the need for those improvements promptly (or even pre-empt them) and ensure that the necessary steps are taken. If there are parts of the new current state that need to be completely redesigned, the change monitor will either oversee that process or actually create another change project to achieve those alterations.

It is not enough merely to monitor the current state to check whether further improvements are needed. All change agents need to accept that, no matter how well they plan the change and how well they implement it, the new current state will take time to gain a firm hold. As the roots of the change bury themselves deep within the structure of the organization, you need to check for "slippage" if you are monitoring the change – the creeping back of old ways. If you delegate this task, agree with the person responsible what measurements or observations they will use to determine whether the new current state is stable.

Perhaps old reporting lines are asserting themselves, or responsibilities are shifting back from one person to another, or even falling by the wayside. A classic example of the latter is a case in which the initiative to obtain cost analyses from the accounts department on a monthly basis and report on project spending in relation to budgets is passed from the creative director to individual project managers. But the project managers feel that they are too busy managing their staff, problem-solving and initiating new projects to worry about how much money they are spending. The idea might have been to free up their time for budget management by having them delegate more of their creative work. But delegating the most creative part of the job is something than most of them are reluctant to do. So the agreed change has foundered, and once again the creative director can only find out whether their spending is on course by liaising with accounts him- or herself.

If you and/or your monitor discover that slippage is occurring in the new current state, you need to take immediate action to resolve it. See the Work Solution opposite for ideas on how to do this.

WORK SOLUTION 19

Dealing with Slippage

If your change project is to succeed in the long term, any "slippage" (return to old, pre-change ways) that occurs in the new current state needs to be resolved as soon as the change monitor spots it happening. This work solution shows you three ways in which to deal with slippage.

1. Decide with the managers how much and what type of slippage falls into the category of "deal with it directly." When that type of slippage occurs, the team leader or manager should speak directly to the people slipping, reminding them of the new current state and of the important reasons for working the new way.

2. If there appears to be a more significant problem – for example, the expenses spreadsheet suddenly has all the old categories in it again and no one feels they really know how much projects are costing – you may want to call a meeting of the disbanded change agents. They need to put together a succinct action plan to tackle the areas of slippage by re-examining the picture of the desired state and reviewing its viability; launching a new communication plan, and perhaps new learning or reward plans. Team leaders and managers should be involved so that they can facilitate the implementation.

3. In extreme circumstances – for example, if the new way in which sales projections feed into the funding of the advertising budget breaks down as a result of poorly designed software – you may need to establish a new change project altogether. To do this, consider the new current state as one that needs to be changed, select change agents (or assign yourself the role) and make them responsible for fixing the problem, treating it like a full-blown change project.

DETERMINING THE EXIT STRATEGY

Your workload is now getting lighter as the old desired state becomes the new current state. Your tasks are almost complete. Your sponsor is content and the targets are starting to accept their changed world as normal. It is time to tie up loose ends and get back to business as usual – or move on to the next change.

It might be tempting to stop right here, as it seems that nobody is watching any more. But bear with us just a little longer: we promise that creating and following an exit strategy is a good idea. If you ever brought your car to the garage for a major service, you are familiar with the exit strategy used by the mechanic. Just before they hand you back the keys, they go through a checklist to be sure that everything was done and everything is in the right place. The purpose of a change exit strategy is similar. It checks that everything was done as the change winds down. In addition, it identifies any risks to the new current state that may still be present.

It's important that you keep a tidy file of all aspects of the change and store this file in a suitable archive – not in deep storage off-site but somewhere more accessible. Bear in mind that the file is meant to be understandable to someone who knows nothing about the change and is coming to it to find out exactly what happened. Spend time ensuring that all the documents are in correct chronological order – after all, time is the medium through which the change has progressed,

WORK SOLUTION 20

Sharing Your Knowledge

By the end of the change process you will have accumulated a mass of documents that the change generated. Now collate all that information into a change-project file. This file will provide the organization with a valuable reference tool that may also be used as a guide for future change projects.

1. Assemble all your documents relating to the change in one file – the analyses of the current state and desired state, the timelines, the communication, learning and reward plans and all the status reports.

2. If you have any documents that exist only as computer files or emails, print them out and file them in the paper change-project file.

3. Given that memories are fallible, and that change is a complex process based on the analysis of a mass of data, the organization will be well served by one-page bullet-point summaries of different aspects and different phases of the change – a separate summary for each group of documents.

4. Provide the file with a contents page that makes it easy to look into any specific aspect of the change.

5. Organize a computer version of the change-project file – or at least of key documents that might be used as templates in the future. Make a note in the paper-version change-project file exactly where the computer version is archived.

6. Ensure that senior managers know where your change-project file is stored.

and a jumbled file does not give a true picture of what actually happened.

People like to know when they have finished a job. They want to know that they have completed their responsibilities and have been given permission (formal or informal) to move on. People also like to know whether the job they have completed was well received. If you were the principal change agent, call one last meeting to give all the other change agents a chance to comment on how the change went. Ask yourselves: What did we do well during this change? What could we do differently in the next change to improve the process? How has the way in which we managed this change taught our organization to do it better next time? How well did the sponsors, the change agents and the targets fulfil their roles and carry out their responsibilities? Next time, will the people who have to change feel more like partners in the change process instead of targets? And so on.

Schedule a final meeting with the sponsor to make sure that they know you are officially finished and to give them the opportunity to comment on the way in which you have handled the change. Reviewing the exit strategy together is a good way to help your sponsor appreciate just how much hard work you have put into making this change successful.

Once all the serious business is out of the way, throw a party to celebrate your achievements. Even if your budget only runs to coffee and doughnuts, make sure that you thank everyone involved and acknowledge all the effort and teamwork that have enabled you to reach your goal.

WORK SOLUTION 21

Closing the Change

One of the most difficult things about being a change agent is to know when and how to stop being one. You have completed this change with thoughtfulness and discipline and can take pride in your approach and your results. Now it's time to close the project and relinquish your change-agent role.

1. Do a personal review of your performance as a change agent. Have you done everything as well as you could? What lessons have you learned about how to make change happen effectively?

2. Talk to the management around you and above you and the people who work for you. Find out if your approach to managing change helped them go through the change. Is there anything more you could have done?

3. Ask yourself if there is any unfinished business that you need to take care of, or pass on to others.

4. Reflect on whether you enjoyed making change happen. If so, you might consider change management as an element of your career development. Ask yourself whether this might be possible within your current organization. Arrange to meet with your boss and have a conversation about your career as an agent of change within the organization.

5. The last step in the exit process is to celebrate the results of all your hard work with any fellow change agents who worked with you. Take collective pride in the efforts you made to make change easier for people and more successful for the organization.

CONCLUSION

If you were embarking on a change project when you picked up this book and worked your way through the chapters, we hope that you applied the change-management strategies and action planning you learned here. If so, the result should have been a positive payback in three ways.

First, your change should have happened faster, more easily, with less stress and disruption and at a lower cost than if you had not applied these approaches. That alone should have been worth all the effort of maximizing support from the sponsor, making sure that the desired state was well explained, building a reward plan, and generally educating and inspiring the workforce into supporting the change.

Second, you, yourself, should have developed skills that add to your personal value within the organization. Change agents who know what they are doing are highly valued in forward-thinking organizations today. They are also much sought after, so you should have increased your own marketability and improved your career prospects too. If you wish to continue to work as a change agent on other changes, your new-found skills will be extremely useful. The more control you have over the change process, the more you get to understand the causes of problems and what to do about them. This, in turn, will make your job as change agent easier and less stressful.

Third, by having managed your change well, you will have contributed to building up a culture of confidence within your organization and will have encouraged the workforce to be more supportive of future changes. The

senior management will not only delight in the fact that changes can happen faster, smoother, easier and more cost-effectively than ever before, they will also realize that the ability to decide to change and then turn this decision into reality gives their organization a key competitive edge.

No serious organization would dream of letting its financial systems operate in a random, unstructured way, because its finances are at the core of its operations. The same applies to change – every organization should take a structured and disciplined approach to change through change management. By using the tools and techniques set out in this book you are laying the foundations for change management to become integral to your organization's operations, thereby contributing to its continued growth and success.

FURTHER READING

Axelrod, Richard and Peter Block *Terms of Engagement: Changing the Way We Change Organizations*, Berrett-Koehler Publishers Inc. (San Francisco), 2001

Buckingham, Marcus and Curt Coffman *First Break All the Rules*, Simon & Schuster (New York), 1999

Cushman, Donald P. and Sarah Sanderson King (eds.) *Communicating Organizational Change: A Management Perspective*, State University of New York Press (Albany, NY), 1995

Daniels, Aubrey C. *Bringing Out the Best in People: How to Apply the Astonishing Power of Positive Reinforcement*, McGraw-Hill (New York), 1999

Deeprose, Donna *How to Recognize and Reward Employees (The Worksmart Series)*, AMACOM (New York), 1994

Galpin, Timothy and Mark Herndon *The Complete Guide to Mergers and Acquisitions: Process Tools to Support M&A Integration at Every Level*, Jossey-Bass Wiley (San Francisco), 1999

Gladwell, Malcolm *The Tipping Point: How Little Things Can Make a Big Difference*, Little, Brown & Co. (New York), 2000 and Abacus (London), 2002

Glanz, Barbara *Care Packages for the Workplace: Dozens of Little Things You Can Do to Regenerate Spirit at Work*, McGraw-Hill Trade (New York), 1996

Goldstein, Jeffrey *The Unshackled Organization: Facing the Challenge of Unpredictability Through Spontaneous Reorganization*, Productivity Press Inc. (New York), 1994

Goleman, Daniel *Working with Emotional Intelligence*, Bantam Books (New York) and Bloomsbury (London), 1998

Jacques, Elliott *Requisite Organization: A Total System for Effective Managerial Organization and Managerial Leadership for the 21st Century*, Cason Hall & Co. Publishing (Gloucester, MA), 1996

Klubnik, Joan P. *Rewarding and Recognizing Employees: Ideas for Individuals, Teams and Managers*, McGraw-Hill Trade (New York), 1996

Kotter, John P. *Leading Change*, Harvard Business School Press (Cambridge, MA), 1996

LaMarsh, Jeanenne *Changing the Way We Change*, Addison-Wesley (Boston, MA), 1995

Larkin, T.J. and Sandra Larkin *Communicating Change: Winning Employee Support for New Business Goals*, McGraw-Hill Trade (New York), 1994

Lundin, Stephen, Harry Paul and John Christensen *Fish! A Remarkable Way to Boost Morale and Improve Results*, Hyperion (New York), 2000

Mellander, Klas *The Power of Learning: Fostering Employee Growth*, McGraw-Hill Trade (New York), 1993

Nelson, Bob and Kenneth Blanchard *1001 Ways to Reward Employees*, Workman Publishing Company (New York), 1994

Scott, Beverly *Consulting on the Inside: An Internal Consultant's Guide*, American Society of Training and Development (Alexandria, VA), 2000

Senge, Peter et al *The Dance of Change: The Challenges to Sustaining Momentum in Learning Organizations*, Doubleday Press (New York), 1999

Smith, Douglas K. *Taking Charge of Change: 10 Principles for Managing People and Performance*, Perseus Publishing (Cambridge, MA), 1996

Smith, Rolf *The 7 Levels of Change: Different Thinking for Different Results*, Tapestry Press (Irving, TX), 1997

Wenger, Etienne, Richard A. McDermott and William Snyder *Cultivating Communities of Practice*, Harvard Business School Press (Cambridge, MA), 2002

Wilson, Thomas *Rewards that Drive High Performance: Success Stories from Leading Organizations*, AMACOM (New York), 1999

INDEX

ACKNOWLEDGMENTS

We would like to thank our clients, who are dedicated to managing their changes and challenging us to bring them new ideas and new insights, as well as improving their capability to make change happen successfully.

CONTACT THE AUTHORS

We would welcome your questions and thoughts about this book and we are interested to hear about your experiences of the change process. Contact us at:

Rebecca Potts
rpotts@lamarsh.com

Jeanenne LaMarsh
jlamarsh@lamarsh.com

http://www.lamarsh.com

LaMarsh & Associates, Inc.
505 N. Lake Shore Drive, Suite 1210
Chicago, IL 60611,
USA
Phone: (312) 464–1349